The Blueprint: Lessons for Living Your Best Life™

The Blueprint:
Lessons for Living Your Best Life
© 2023 by BK Fulton

ISBN (E-book) : 978-1-949929-96-6
ISBN (Paperback) : 978-1-949929-94-2
ISBN (Hardback) : 978-1-949929-95-9

Owl Publishing, LLC.

150 Parkview Heights Road, Ephrata PA 17522

717-925-7511

www.owlpublishinghouse.com

Published in the United States of America

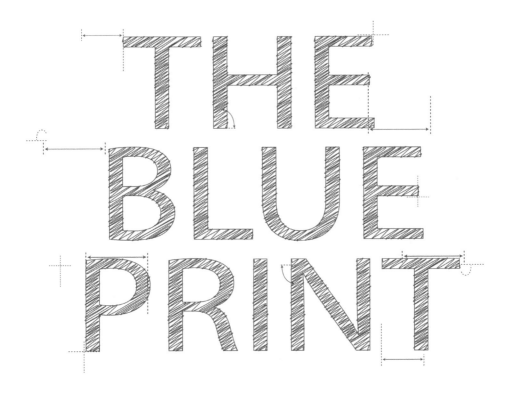

BK FULTON

Lessons For Living Your Best Life

FOREWORD

It has been my great privilege over the last few years to serve as the co-founding editor of SoulVision Magazine. We created SoulVision to highlight as much human excellence as possible for as long as we were able to run the monthly magazine. We started the venture with hopes that we might run for 2-3 years. We ended up publishing the magazine for 4 years and growing it to 150,000 subscribers. Each month we shared stories of creatives, leading entrepreneurs, community leaders and culinary wizards. As co-editor, each month I would write what we called an "Editor's Note" to summarize the contents of each issue. One some occasions, Mr. Nicholas Powell, my co-founding editor, would write the monthly editor's note. Collectively, we penned 48 notes and several hundred articles that we distributed digitally around the globe.

When we decided to suspend the magazine at the end of 2022, we realized that the first-class content could serve as a blessing for anyone hoping to be inspired by the best from our collective communities. Many of our subscribers asked us to continue to update them on our film, stage, movie and media investment projects. We are doing that. Additionally, the idea of writing this book – *The Blueprint* – came from our readers. They asked us to share the "secret sauce" for how we are able to produce so much content (20 films, 16 books, two number one Broadway shows, a popular magazine and a cable network, among other media investments). As we looked back over our work, we realized that the stories in the magazine, particularly the editor's notes, contained the secret sauce. This secret sauce guided our success as a company and showcased a path for our readers to live their best lives.

This book is a collection of the raw editor's notes as published in SoulVision magazine from 2019 to 2022. These four years summarize the work of our team and my thoughts over the course of the four-year life of the magazine. Also included are select speeches and writings that I have shared over the years. These expressions chronicle my thinking from my early days as a young leader focused on finding my way here in US to a wiser citizen of the world interested in the best for all of humanity. I hope this book inspires you as much as creating it has inspired me. Love is the secret ingredient.

With Love,

TABLE OF CONTENTS

SOULVISION MAGAZINE EDITOR'S NOTES

2019

2020

2021

2022

SPEECHES 118
1992-2020

Our greatest accomplishments lie on the other side of our fears. My prayer for each of you is that you love yourself enough to give your dreams a chance.

BK FULTON

DEC 2018/JAN 2019

"One key to making good art is being open to the order inherent in the chaos of our lives. No key is wrong when the feeling is right. As I learned more, I gave up on trying to find perfection. I trust that God will order my steps as long as I am present. In other words, we just need to do the work!"

- BK FULTON

"EACH DAY IS A GIFT. WHAT YOU DO WITH IT IS YOUR GIFT BACK."

In his condo, overlooking the financial district of Downtown Richmond on one side and the James River on the other, BK Fulton is restless; he's wrestling with an idea, a vision that will serve as an extension of Soulidifly Productions, where he serves as founding chairman and CEO. Fragments are beginning to take shape as tangible ideas. He walks back and forth and then he stops and looks out at his patio. He feels the ancestors are laughing at him with love as he realizes that it's up to him to tell the stories that have not been told. "SoulVision," he utters and that was it. In less than a week, he finds a founding editor, web developers and designers, lawyers to protect the name and a band of contributing authors. In a world where black and brown people are too often thought of as less than, BK created SoulVision to exemplify the positive energy inherent in urban communities worldwide.

BK doesn't shy away from making it known that Soulidifly Productions is the first independent film company in cinema history to produce and release four feature-length films in its first year. Produced by a mostly unknown team of diverse industry insiders and creatives, these films include Charniece Fox's *Love Dot Com*, Menelek Lumumba's *1 Angry Black Man*, and Wes Miller's River *Runs Red* and *Atone*. With respectable offers from major movie producers in the film and paid TV business, there is only one way to go but up for Soulidify Productions.

Known for his positive outlook on life, BK believes that "God blesses us all to turn our dreams and ideas into their tangible equivalents; we must have the faith, be willing to do the work and expect the outcomes." With a team of talented folks behind him, BK has the recipe for phenomenal success.

FEBRUARY 2019

"Start where you are, use what you have and do what you can!" ARTHUR ASHE

We stand on the shoulders of many unsung heroes and sheroes who survived on faith, hope and love so that one day we could manifest the promise of our creation. This month, we've asked some of the best in the music business to share their stories and inspirations with our readers. In each case, a humility comes through that is tangible. It's as if a divine serendipity unfolded in our pages. We pray that this issue of

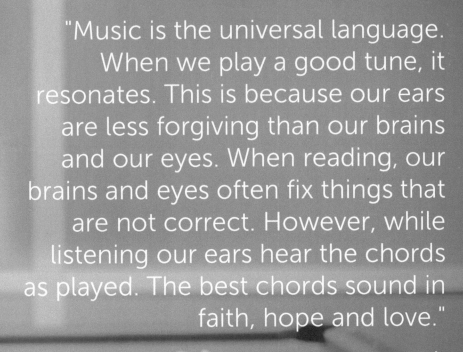

"Music is the universal language. When we play a good tune, it resonates. This is because our ears are less forgiving than our brains and our eyes. When reading, our brains and eyes often fix things that are not correct. However, while listening our ears hear the chords as played. The best chords sound in faith, hope and love."

- BK

SoulVision Magazine brings you into proximity with the person you were made to be. When we draw on the lessons and courage of others to do what was necessary in their times, we often find blueprints and guidance to push through the trials of our times. Last, while it's true that we stand on the shoulders of giants, we must remember that we are standing here, not to be seen, but instead to see the way forward for the next generation. Our lives must reflect who we should be; who we are blessed to be; and who we were made to be. Go forward unafraid with SoulVision.

MARCH 2019

"Divine serendipity happens when God places us in proximity to those we need to work with to give love a chance." - *BK*

"ALL OF US SHOULD STRIVE TO BE EXCELLENT."

Fate rarely calls upon us at a moment of our own choosing. The opportunity for each of us to be great is preserved for those who are prepared. This issue of SoulVision Magazine focuses on the storytellers, the talent that brings stories to life, and those who produce and train the next generations of movie and media professionals. The creators in this issue were inspired by nature, family stories and their God-given talents, to create art at the highest levels. The pursuit of excellence inspired them to dig and press on until their stories were told.

So it is with each of us, we have to be willing to do what it takes to evolve into the people we are supposed to be.

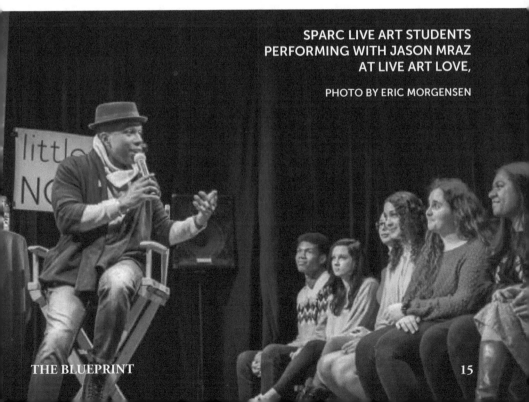

SPARC LIVE ART STUDENTS PERFORMING WITH JASON MRAZ AT LIVE ART LOVE,

PHOTO BY ERIC MORGENSEN

"The rearview mirror has so much less to offer than the windshield facing the open road in front of you. Don't focus on failures, learn and be better as you go forward."

– BK Fulton

APRIL 2019

"We stand on the shoulders of giants, not to be
seen, but to see the best path ahead to help those
who must follow."

WE ALL HAVE BEEN INSPIRED BY SOMETHING BEAUTIFUL.
When we hear a certain note that gives us goosebumps, watch
an actor deliver a perfect line, or get teary-eyed when those we
love do their best through an expressive form, we experience the
great moments of humanity.

Art shapes our culture. The clearest path to a better world is built
on a foundation of excellence in all that we choose to do.

CHOOSE TO BE EXCELLENT BY DESIGN.

When you pursue something with excellence, the best results
tend to come out. My advice to young people is to be excellent
by design—that's number one. And number two, you don't have
to reinvent the wheel while you are figuring out how to get
from where you are to where you want to be. You can read the
biographies of three or four people you respect and follow their
plan—which is what I did. When you read those biographies—and
you can read the short version—see what they did, lay out the
common denominators of their success and mirror that. It will
often go like this—go to college, get an internship, get a job, find
mentors, work at this place and that place. You can use someone
else's plan and eventually, add your own nuances and interests
as you discover them. But please remember, it is important for
you to develop your own plan and write it down.

When I was in engineering and architecture school at
Virginia Tech over 30 years ago, I wrote a 50-year plan.
What I've been doing ever since then is executing that plan
and checking off boxes. If something came up that didn't
contribute to my plan, I didn't do it; and if it contributed to
my plan, I would consider it and might do it. The point here
is that I had written it down. I had a standard of excellence.
I used the blueprints of others until I could add my own
scaffolding to my plan. This has worked for me, and now
I find myself in a position to use the power of art to help
other people find things that inspire them.

MAY 2019

"Take the first step in the right direction and change the world."

This issue of SoulVision Magazine focuses on leadership and how it can shape and influence art. Humans take pride when someone "steps up" for an important cause. Whether it is a leader like Rosa Parks who decided that sitting down

"Nothing beats a failure except a try. Perfection is not required."

- BK Fulton

wherever she pleased after a full day's work was right, or Barak Obama addressing the world from the oval office in a time that required unity, leaders emerge and often inspire. Artists capture great moments in the human story when they sing, write, and innovate about leaders. Our world can become even better when we lead or follow leaders and work on just causes together. The leaders in our May issue are among the lesser known and yet important influencers in the world who have chosen to do the meaningful work that benefits generations.

We hope their lives and example will inspire all.

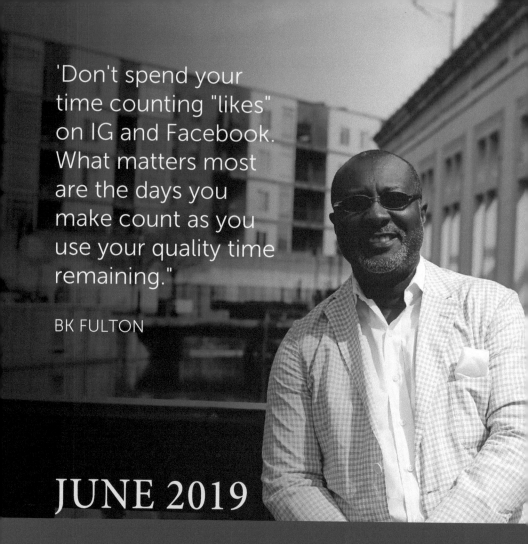

'Don't spend your time counting "likes" on IG and Facebook. What matters most are the days you make count as you use your quality time remaining."

BK FULTON

JUNE 2019

We are all really one race that shares the same rock."

2019 marks the 400th anniversary of the arrival of enslaved Africans to America. Many scholars assert that long before 1619, African travelers explored the world as evidenced by writings, carvings, and artifacts found throughout the world. While our planet continues to get smaller with great advances in technology and the way we communicate via e-mail, text and other applications, we still find that human relations have not advanced as much as we would hope. Sure, there is substantial progress from what our ancestors faced long ago in this land. However, it is critically important that today's truth seeker is exposed to all of the stories that teach us who we are and what it means to be a human being. After all, we are really one race that shares the same rock.

Our collective interest represents our core strength.

In this issue of SoulVision Magazine, we talk to some of the new storytellers and artists who are using their talents to lift as we all climb.

"God does not bless us because we are good: God blesses us because she is good."

In this issue of SoulVision Magazine, we focus on entrepreneurs. The creators and makers featured here use their art to build communities and to turn the wheels of commerce. Our ancestors knew that self-sufficiency was a prerequisite for long-term survival in a world where green and gold were the most important colors. Historically, our dollars circulated hundreds of times in our own community ecosystem. Today, a dollar spent in urban communities barely circulates one time before it goes out to enrich other neighborhoods. According to the Opportunity HUB (OHUB), in 2013 the median wealth of White families was $134,000, Black families' median wealth was $11,000 and all U.S. families had a median wealth of $81,000. The same report went on to share that only 1% of Blacks were worth more than $1 million dollars (compared to 12% of Whites) and 30% of Blacks were worth $50,000 to $1 million dollars (compared to 55% of Whites). There is a clear wealth gap between ethnicities. What's more, that gap is becoming a chasm when you consider that 27% of African Americans have a *negative* net worth (compared to 9% of Whites).

These differences impact more than finances. Wealth gaps also impact opportunities, education, and perceptions. "Lack" can become a pernicious cycle. In an age where we ostensibly and in fact have more freedom, more resources, and more education than any generation of African Americans in the U.S., we are doing less building than we have in generations. Why? One hypothesis is that urban communities are not doing all they can to support each other and work collectively to make our U.S. and global standing better. It is time to do more than survive. It is time to develop and prosper. SoulVision Magazine salutes the entrepreneurs who are working hard to achieve each and every one of their dreams. Remember to lift as you climb . . . , together.

"There is a clear wealth gap between ethnicities. What's more, that gap is becoming a chasm. . . ."

AUGUST 2019

"The butterfly is beautiful and free only because the caterpillar is courageous and brave."

The Atlantic slave trade was one of the most evil and pernicious assaults on humanity that the world has ever experienced. In just 315 years, tens-of-millions of Africans were kidnapped from Africa and taken in ships—more than 20,500 known voyages—to be worked to death in foreign lands. The perpetrators of these crimes against humanity did everything in their power to justify the trade of human flesh on this massive scale. They even went on in an attempt to further dehumanize their captives by saying they were sub-human and that God had ordained the practice. Of course, these notions are untrue and represent humanity at its lowest point. Through the valiant efforts of many over the same period of years, the tide turned and the practice of human bondage and trafficking as a legal activity was outlawed and over time, defeated. While our world still has illegal forms of trafficking and human bondage, little compares to the years between 1583 and 1883, when our ancestors were ripped from their homes and kingdoms to build other nations. What amazes me is how resilient our ancestors were, even in the face of pure evil. They chose to survive so that future generations might thrive once again.

In this issue of SoulVision Magazine, we focus on artists across the Atlantic who bring forth what is beautiful in the world, notwithstanding very challenging common origins. There is still much work to do before we can reclaim even a fraction of what was lost. However, doing the work continues to be the message to all humanity. The world needs more love. The world needs more soul. Welcome to SoulVision Magazine for August.

"Our ancestors chose to survive so that future generations may thrive . . . ."

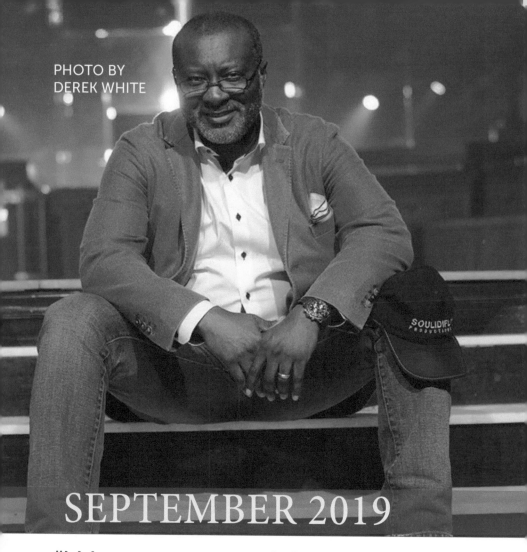

SEPTEMBER 2019

"We must position our children for their purpose..."

It is important to live our best lives. We become who we become by continuously learning, working and sharing. The notion of "self-made" is incomplete without acknowledgment and thanks to those who have helped us along the way. There is always someone who helped. There is always a seed that is planted, and it must be cared for if it is to grow. Thirty years ago, I was in Cambridge finishing the second summer of a Sloan Fellowship. The experience changed my life. I went from the academic probation list at Virginia Tech to tutoring statistics and economics at Harvard. I subsequently accepted a full ride to the Milano Graduate School of Management and International Policy before earning my law degree a few years later. The rest is history.

I worked at the National Urban League, AOL, Time Warner, the U.S. Department of Commerce and then Verizon. I retired in 2015 and wrote my first book, *Shauna*, about my youngest sister. I found my soulmate and started and/or chair seven companies. We are working on our seventh feature film and our company owns a digital TV network, and a digital magazine, and will release 7-10 books this year. We mentor and coach 7-25 young leaders each year. We have a scholarship that helps talented youth pay for school. We are blessed and happy. At every turn and every bump in the road, someone helped me as I learned to help myself. I now fully understand the importance and the power of working together to make our world a better place.

Accordingly, we dedicate this issue of SoulVision Magazine to the "makers" who created something out of what seemed to be nothing. They are writers, motivational speakers, choreographers, actors, designers, and iconographers. In their own way, each one is blazing a path forward. In most cases, they worked their way into their dreams and our lives. They inspire us to be better; the best version of ourselves. Pray every day. Be thankful every day. Work smarter every day. God is in the details. Welcome to the September Issue of SoulVision Magazine.

"There is always someone who helped . . . ."

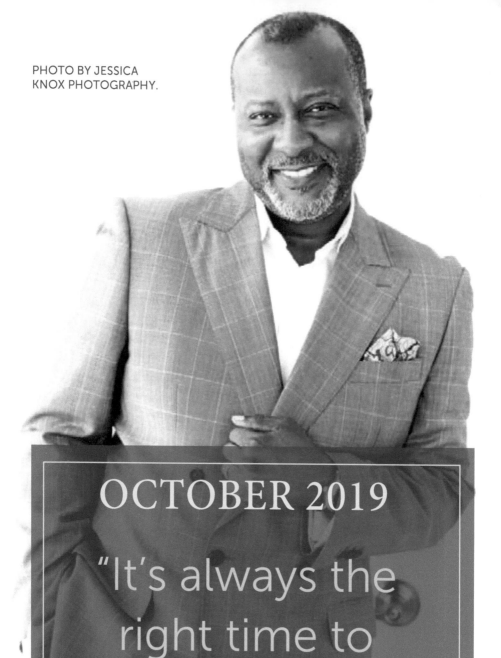

OCTOBER 2019

"It's always the
right time to
be kind . . . ."

Recently, I was moved almost to tears as I read about a little boy who loved the University of Tennessee/UT so much that he drew a design of the school's logo on paper and pinned it to his shirt for "College Colors Day" at his elementary school. He was teased by some students who did not even participate in the school pride day. His excitement was crushed and he went home to his mom in tears. A teacher decided to post the ordeal on social media. Supportive notes of love and UT pride started coming in from all over. The University also sent him a care package and decided to make his shirt an official selection at the VolShop—their store for ordering UT gear. Pre-orders for the shirt crashed the VolShop commerce site with some 50,000 orders and counting. Some of the proceeds for the sale of the young man's "U.T." shirt will go to an anti-bullying foundation. Further, UT has offered the young man a scholarship in 2032!

I am convinced that if we can teach hate and meanness, we can teach love and kindness. In this special issue of SoulVision Magazine, we try out a new cover story format and focus on creators who love what they do so much that they have become new innovators in old spaces. We even take the covers off the creative souls working to deliver Soulidifly Productions (creators of SoulVision Magazine and SoulVision. TV). Enjoy . . . and don't forget to choose kindness and love. You get a new look when you have SoulVision.

> "If we can teach hate and meanness, we can teach love and kindness."

NOVEMBER 2019

"Each day is a gift...,
what you do with it is
your gift back."

Thanks to our readers, it has been a great year for SoulVision Magazine. Your sharing and spreading the word about SoulVision Magazine has helped us to expand our global reach. In this issue, we continue with our new cover format. The lead story about Marc Randolph and how he co-founded Netflix is a must-read. We also highlight the beautiful images of Ms. Jessica Knox. Finally, we salute the one and only Queen Latifah who was in town hosting a summit on women achievers. In other words, we are closing out the year bringing it, just like we started. You get a new look when you have SoulVision! Thank you and enjoy.

"We are closing out the year ...just like we started."

"Entrepreneurs are the problem-solvers of today."

NETFLIX CO-FOUNDER MARC RANDOLPH

PHOTO BY PAUL RIEDMILLER

Kehinde Wiley & Valerie Cassel Oliver.

"The world is waiting to hear your voice and see your art."

VALERIE CASSEL OLIVER:

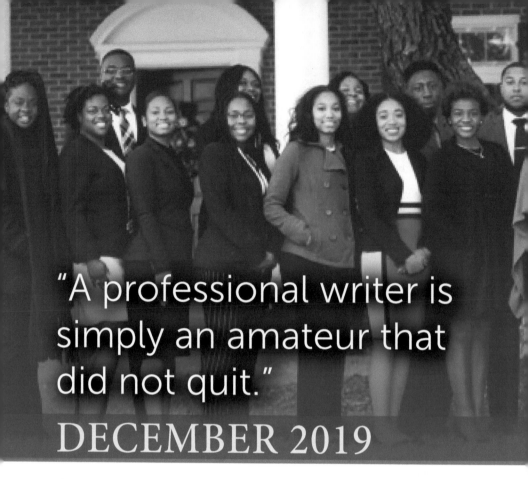

"A professional writer is simply an amateur that did not quit."

DECEMBER 2019

This week has been a whirlwind for the team at Soulidifly Productions (producers of SoulVision Magazine). We did TV interviews about the *Mr. Business* book series and we spoke at leadership programs and community programs about our work. We released a film, Love Dot Com: The Social Experiment, worldwide on Blu-ray and video-on-demand (VOD) and we will release another film, Hell on the Border, on December 13 with Lionsgate! The team at SoulVision Magazine realized that our 2019 was a year of plenty. We did the work and we thank our readers for telling the world about us.

I am particularly proud of one of our youngest readers, Chance (age 4), who joined us for a wonderful night of reading and sharing in Norfolk, Virginia thanks to Clever Communities In Action (CCIA). It was at that same event

where I was asked about writing and where do you start . . . I told them to just write. Get out a pen or pencil and a pad and start writing your story. That's how we started this magazine. The stories we shared in SoulVision Magazine are a taste of what's on deck for next year. Please enjoy this "year in review" from SoulVision Magazine and a clip from our young readers event at Clever Communities In Action. Support our young people as we prepare them for their purpose. Have a joyous holiday season and we'll see you in 2020 – You get a new look when you have SoulVision!

"Support our young people as we prepare them for their purpose."

JANUARY 2020

"Thoughts come before things."

Welcome back for another year of SoulVision Magazine. We kick off 2020 with the amazing story of Christy Coleman, incoming leader of the Jamestown-Yorktown Foundation and former leader of the American Civil War Museum. Christy was named one of the "31 people changing the South" by *Time* magazine. She is a pioneer and reminds us

of the irony that "history is about how we are living in the present." As we were putting together this issue, I was reminded of what I had to let go in order to be where I am today. Before this uplift I had to go through the process of an upshift. My habits, friends, actions and faith all had to change for the best me to become what God intended for me to be. I AM grateful for my journey.

As we begin another fruitful year, it is important that we give our youth a fighting chance. If they don't learn, we did not teach. Thoughts come before things. Assemble the youth and show them how to turn their dreams and ideas into their tangible equivalents. We are the way. Become the change you seek .... one race: humans. One reason: LOVE.

"If [our children] don't learn, we did not teach."

FEBRUARY 2020

"If you have a vision in your heart, . . . act on it."

If you have something to say, . . . say it. If you have a song within you, . . . sing it. If you have a book in you, . . . write it. The artists and leaders we profile in our February issue are making the world better by doing what they were born to do. They have figured out a way to get out of their own way and to just do it. I hope you enjoy reading about their journey and learning from their examples. The cover feature on Paul Goodnight is nothing short of amazing. He lays out his

"The world is a place where our efforts make our dreams come true."™

metamorphosis into an internationally known and respected powerhouse of creative expression. His art moves all who see it. The story of Kitt Shapiro (daughter of the late great Eartha Kitt) is a reminder that "the fruit don't fall far from the tree." Plunky brings the funk and Maggie Small reminds us that there is power in grace. The storied ballerina is still doing what she loves. That's the lesson right . . . do what you love. All of these pioneers and innovators remind us of what is possible and that love is the secret ingredient. I love that you have chosen to read SoulVision Magazine. I love that each day is a new opportunity to be better. I love that you get a new look when you have SoulVision.

MARCH 2020

> "Stories of achievement and overcoming obstacles in life have been rocket fuel for my soul."

What would it be like to have 1,000 books in your pocket? As you know, the editors of SoulVision Magazine believe that readers become leaders. In this month's issue, we feature an insightful interview with Max Tuchman, founding CEO of Caribu.com. Caribu was named one of the "100 Best Inventions of 2019" by *TIME Magazine*. The app allows caring adults to read and draw with kids in real-time from anywhere in the world! They have over 1,000 titles for readers to choose from, including all 7 of the *Mr. Business* books. Max shares what it's like to be a female innovator and leader who happens to be of Latinx and Jewish heritage. Max is so confident in Caribu that she gives away the monthly subscription service to active U.S. service men and women. She is putting 1,000 kids' books in our pockets and connecting families around the globe. Our March issue also shines a light on first-time feature film director Brett Smith who is currently filming *Freedom's Path*. The film takes place in the Antebellum South at the dawn of the Civil War. *Freedom's Path* is a story of friendship and what it really takes to be courageous. March is National Reading Month.

This month we also highlight the great Willie Lanier in our living legends story. The Hall of Famer took some time with us because he is an avid reader. Willie notes that reading changed his life. Tackle Reading, founded by Kathryn Stark, is our community feature this month. Tackle Reading partners with over 32 NFL teams, alumni chapters and NFL greats like Roger Staubach and Willie Lanier to read to kids for Tackle Reading Day on the 2nd day of March. *Mr. Business* will be a part of this year's program that will reach tens of thousands of kids from coast to coast.

I will have the pleasure of reading to nearly 700 kids in Virginia with Willie Lanier, considered one of the 100 best professionals to ever play in the NFL. The library is a special place to me. Reading changed my life too. Stories of achievement and overcoming obstacles in life have been rocket fuel for my soul. Reading about the accomplishments of others continues to serve as a blueprint for my journey and a beacon for what is possible. Thank you Ron Brown, Dick Parsons, Marianne Spraggins, and Vernon Jordan for showing me the way with your examples.

> "One of the most important things our young people need today to achieve their best lives is having accessible, courageous and supportive mentors and role models. **Be one.**"

APRIL 2020

"...do it from a place of love."

When we started SoulVision Magazine in late 2018, there were many naysayers who questioned if the world was ready for another publication. We took that leap of faith and now our articles are read by over 100,000 people each month, and we are reprinted and distributed in over 261 cities around the globe. This issue is our way of saying thank you to all of our readers and supporters. In this issue, we continue to bring light and love by showcasing a pioneering young leader who is vegan, a business leader, a fitness professional, and a motivational speaker. Yes, I'm talking about the sensational, albeit lesser-known, Brandi Harvey. Her cover story will amaze you. We also have the good fortune of featuring Ken Harvey, former NFL superstar turned creative writing phenomena. Filmmaker Lauren Meyer and artist Acori Honzo are in this month's issue. Buckle up! We plan to keep pushing as we bring you a new look with SoulVision.

THOUGHTS ON CORONA

When COVID-19 hit, we realized that we could not stop our work to lift others with positive and inspirational stories. Even with all the madness in the world, we should continue to smile. Why? Because you woke up. When we have the gift of life, we have the promise of hope and the lift of faith. Hope is our comfort in the storm. Faith is our guide in the night. The two combined allow us to make a way out of no way. Accordingly, no matter the circumstances, let's all choose to live each day rejoicing! The resources below may be helpful as you self-quarantine to project yourself, your family and the world:

FREE CLASSES – Currently, all eight Ivy Leagues— Brown, Harvard, Cornell, Princeton, Dartmouth, Yale, Columbia, and the University of Pennsylvania—are offering 450 active, free courses across a range of topics digitally. All you have to do is visit Class Central – https://www.classcentral.com/, find the area of study you're most interested in and sign up through that university's website.

FREE AUDIO BOOKS – Audible, my favorite audiobook company, just announced that a large selection of audiobooks will be available to anyone for free for as long as the schools are closed. Enjoy! www.stories.audible.com. Free Online Library,

ART AND VIDEO CHAT – Caribu, one of the best inventions of 2019 according to Time Magazine, is allowing FREE and UNLIMITED access to their app for all families and any caring adults who would like to read live to children impacted by the coronavirus pandemic. Caribu allows kids to read and draw in a real-time video-call with family and friends. Tap the link to download the app and read our *"Mr. Business"* series and over 1,000 other great children's books (http://bit.ly/download-caribu) for free as we fight COVID-19.

Soulidifly Productions, the parent company of SoulVision Magazine, keeps pushing the envelope. We launched SoulVision.TV on all major platforms (Apple TV, Roku, Amazon Fire) and all mobile devices in the first quarter of 2020 – on Valentine's Day. We released our first international film, Joseph, in Nigeria and Ghana, and partnered with AMC to release the film in select theaters in the US. The book series, *Mr. Business*, also made its debut on Caribu.com, the world's leading video read-along app. Finally, our romantic comedy feature film, *Love Dot Com: The Social Experiment,* continues to do well on Netflix. We thank everyone who supports the work. We do it from a place of love. Stay safe and remember a positive attitude is contagious too.

MAY 2020

"... explore the little things in life and the big ones too."

Our May issue is dedicated to those who inspire. We feature Tai Babilonia, Kelcey Mawema, Rolonda Wright, Daphne Maxwell Reid and other creators whose work lifts us. We also were fortunate to spend this month with the amazing Adriana Trigiani – author, director, historian ... and renaissance woman! Adriana graces our May cover because she is an example of the best of us and yet she remains as humble as her origins. Big Stone Gap, also the name of her first movie, is Adriana's hometown where she grew up with grace and the support of her family. It was there that she explored the little things in life and the big ones too. Reading and learning were the driving forces behind her creativity. She thought she was going to be a poet until telling stories as an author became her passion. I was so moved by our interview with Adriana, that I wrote a poem in her honor (see below). Thank you, Adriana and all of our guests for this issue of SoulVision Magazine. You get a new look when you have SoulVision

A LIGHT OF THE WORLD

Raised right and beautiful too . . .
the world is better because of you!
Keep on doing the things that you do;
don't let the naysayers say when you're through.
Make them learn as much as you teach . . .
you are changing our nation and the world is in reach!
Remember the babies; it's about them not us.
Their eyes will keep twinkling when they hear "truth"
they can trust.
Last, but not least . . . don't take no crap!
Because a light of the world is from Big Stone Gap!

BK FULTON

"Even with all the madness in the world, we should continue to smile."

JUNE 2020

"Where there is God, there is ALWAYS a way."

Whether you are 19 or over 50, the biggest battle you will ever fight is the one you fight with yourself to become who you are supposed to be. My kids always wanted me to teach them to punch and kick. I told them first they had to learn to be still and silent. When you can't go outside, the strong know how to go inside. When you think there is no way, the wise know how to invoke the ultimate way maker. Where there is God, there is ALWAYS a way. None of us need to be a Super-Man to be great. However, it helps to have a Super-Plan if you want to become the best version of yourself. Stay strong. Embrace the flow of the Almighty. Your breakthrough is on the other side of your struggles. Have faith that this season shall pass with you standing. In this

PHOTO BY TIMOTHY STEPHENSON

issue of SoulVision Magazine, we focus on creators and leaders who have broken through something to get where they are. Rob Chesnut, Chief Ethics Officer of Airbnb, shares an amazing story of corporate enlightenment. Larry Palmer reminds us that perseverance is the key to a meaningful life. Dr. Joanne Veal Gabbin reveals her journey to poetic excellence. Her husband, Dr. Alexander Gabbin, crushed boundaries to create the first black MBA association. He is this month's Living Legend. We also are excited to announce the release of a new film — the award-winning 1 Angry Black Man by first-time writer/director Menelek Lumumba. The producers and filmmakers have asked black men and others worldwide to share an image of themselves smiling with a "#1angryblackman" sign and a short story of how they break through stereotypes. The film releases this month on all digital platforms and DVD (June 5, 2020). Finally, artist and illustrator phenom Salaam Muhammad showcases a new online store and his ability to do commissions and reproductions in volume. These breakthroughs are a direct result of doing the work. Enjoy our June issue. You get a new look when you have SoulVision.

Remember, wear your mask and wash your hands.
We will get through this together.

"Your breakthrough is on the other side of your struggles. Have faith that this season shall pass with you standing."

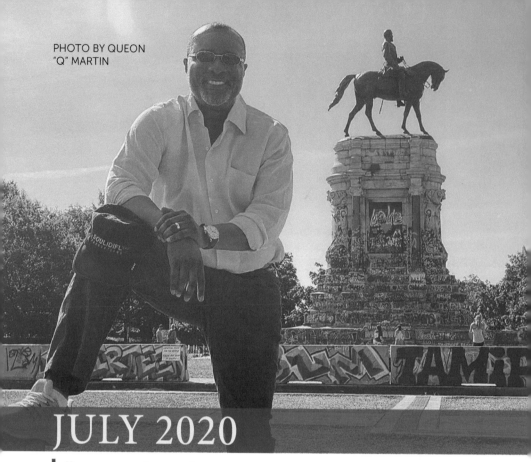

JULY 2020

"...only the truth will set us free."

Over the course of 50+ years of being American and Virginian, I have learned that we are all simply human beings sharing the same rock. I try to teach my children and friends who will listen that we are all cousins trying to find our way home. I also teach my sons that while they should enjoy the same rights and privileges as others, the reality is that they live in a nation that is not well. The sickness created by a culture that would rather teach lies about Christopher Columbus than acknowledge truths about Lewis H. Latimer (the Virginian son of runaway slaves who invented the filament for the present-day light bulb), means my sons exist in a world that does not always protect the value of their humanity. A culture that overplays white contributions and underplays the contributions of people of color will underplay the importance of who they are as young black men. The educational and political systems of our Land, formal and informal, have too often perpetuated a Eurocentric indoctrination of humanity versus teaching critical thinking. It is up to civil society to close the gap between the two. This is where the "truth" lives ... in the gap. It is only the truth that will set us free.

This issue of SoulVision Magazine focuses on healing. You will hear a great word from author and Pastor Jacqui Coles. Her story of rejuvenation and spiritual awakening is powerful. Similarly, Keisha Green's story reminds us to never give up. No excuses. We decided that comfort food should be on deck in this issue so we have a great recipe from Lynn Painter and some off-the-chain good soul mixes from Mrs. Glynis Albright. Finally, we showcase several artists who are bringing it with messages and images that are ripe for the times. Award-winning director Menelek Lumumba is tearing up the film industry with his debut film *1 Angry Black Man*. We can't say enough about it. One national critic wrote that the film was *"the most important film release"* [in June]. Stacy Spikes, founder of urbanworld – the largest multicultural film festival in the world – put the film in his top 10 films to watch for real change. We close out our look at amazing artists with a story on HKB FiNN and folk-artist William A. Floyd. Thank you for selecting our magazine. You get a new look when you have SoulVision.

"We are all simply human beings sharing the same rock."

Stacy Spikes Watch List

1. The Hate You Give
2. When They See Us
3. Harriet
4. Just Mercy
5. Get Out
6. BlacKkKlansman
7. Loving
8. If Beale Street Could Talk
9. 1 Angry Black Man
10. Queen and Slim

AUGUST 2020

"No man is perfect and fate does not call upon us at a moment of our own choosing."

We lost the pioneering civil rights activist C.T. Vivian and the great champion for justice John Lewis on the same day in July. The two men were friends. We were set to run Rev. Vivian's quote in our *Living Legends* section of SoulVision Magazine. We decided to run it anyway as well as a quote from John Lewis. Additionally, we are changing the name of the Living Legends section to *"Legends"* in honor of these civil rights icons. Here we will honor those past and present who are champions for justice and examples of being the best versions of ourselves. In this issue, we also shine a spotlight on music genius Eric Darius, who uses his talent and new record label to change lives. The phenomenal artistry of Steve Prince is also showcased in this issue along with newcomer Josh Mervin, who is making waves with his nexus between sports, art and culture. Last, Tiffany Jana tells us what we need to know to get our minds right and Chef Onwauchi shows us what to do to get our hunger satisfied. There is a lot of love in our August issue.

Remember, the path to where we are today is full of flawed characters: LBJ, even though a Southern Dixiecrat, led the charge for much-needed civil rights and voting rights legislation in the 60s; Hugo Black, although a Klan sympathizer, joined the Supreme Court majority in <u>Brown v. Board of Education</u> (1954); and Abraham Lincoln, although he would debate Douglass to the end on the inferiority of the enslaved, pushed for the Emancipation Proclamation that freed them (1863). No man is perfect and fate does not call upon us at a moment of our own choosing. I pray that when we get our moment, flaws and all, we step up into the role God has blessed us to undertake. The sickness of racism and bigotry cannot sustain the constant antibiotic drip of united citizens operating in the cause of justice and righteousness. It may take longer than any of us desire, but I am optimistic that as each of us brings our best selves to the fight for what is right, we can make this world a better place. In other words, I love you . . . flaws and all. Check out the new Hidden Beach music from the Grammy Award-winning artist BeBe Winans. Proceeds will be donated to Black Lives Matter and Bryan Stevenson's Equal Justice Initiative.

The Tale of the Tee, co-authored by BK Fulton and Jonathan Blank, will be available to purchase at online bookstores early this month.

CO-AUTHORS BK FULTON (RIGHT) AND JONATHAN BLANK. PHOTO BY QUEON "Q" MARTIN.

SEPTEMBER 2020

"What are the conversations we need to have today?"

Recently, we were blessed with a commissioned gift of figurines from the great Acori Honzo. He sent us images of Martin Luther King, Jr. and Malcolm X. The surreal life-like figurines are arranged in a conversation on a park bench somewhere in America. What would they talk about today? They started out in very different places and before they were assassinated in '65 (Malcolm) and '68 (King), their views had become very similar. What are the conversations we need to have today? Thank you Acori Honzo for making these for Soulidifly Productions. Check out our latest project – a book about two men becoming friends after a conversation. Be sure to get your copy of The Tale of the Tee. We each can become the change we seek. In this issue we keep the conversations going with the amazing story of a man who was destined to lead. Dr. Chris Howard is the President of Robert Morris University (RMU) in Pittsburgh, Pennsylvania. Prior to this appointment, he was the President of Hampden-Sydney College in Hampden-Sydney, Virginia, and one of the youngest university presidents in the nation. We also feature Sean Powell, a social innovator who is bringing a new kind of cool to social justice, we check out the wines of Theodora Lee, we chat with newcomer and lifestyle influencer Avery Banks, and take a closer look at the work of Emmy-winning filmmaker Loki Mulholland. Finally, we keep the recognition of achievement going with a quote from Charles Reynolds, the first African-American federal bank examiner in the history of the United States. Thank you for reading our magazine. You get a new look when you have SoulVision!

MARTIN LUTHER KING, JR. AND MALCOLM X HAVE A CONVERSATION ON A PARK BENCH SOMEWHERE IN AMERICA.
FIGURINES BY ACORI HONZO. PHOTO BY QUEON "Q" MARTIN.

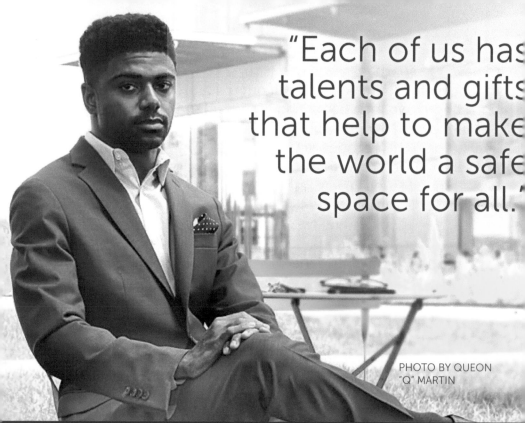

> "Each of us has talents and gifts that help to make the world a safe space for all."

OCTOBER 2020

We will all be telling our children, grandchildren, and great-grandchildren what it was like living in America in 2020. Is it too much to say that we are exhausted? I know I am. Breonna Taylor was only 26 years old when she was murdered. Ahmaud Arbery was 25 years old when he was murdered. I am 25. When you think about your own mortality, the deaths of your peers start to weigh on you. Over 200,000 Americans have died from COVID-19. As a country, we are under the leadership of a man who has threatened a coup if he does not win the presidential election. John Lewis is gone. C.T. Vivian is gone. I look at my peers and the generation behind me and wonder what the future will be like for us. As our parents and grandparents age and retire, we will be in leadership roles, creating laws and building communities and families of our own. We are the change.

We have marched in the streets. We have torn down statues. In some municipalities, we have changed laws. In November, we elect not just the president. Depending on where you live, your ballot may include a vote for mayor, sheriff, district attorney, judges, governor, your state legislator, and your senator and representative in Congress. In November, we vote for everything that matters.

Here is an excellent resource from the New York Times on what you need to do to make sure your voice is heard: https://nyti.ms/3cDdEUU. In this issue of SoulVision Magazine, our cover story is founder and co-founding editor BK Fulton. He shares with us his vision for Soulidifly Productions' future and what lessons he hopes we will learn in the midst of America's racial awakening. Elsewhere, we honor social justice advocate and leader Dr. Iva E. Carruthers. Also in this issue, DeNita Turner helps us to stay positive, NFL vet Antoine Bethea supports families facing evictions, fashion designer Alvin Thompson designs eco-friendly fashion for all, Louise Keeton writes stories that educate and empower, and Kristen Peyton creates beautiful art for some much-needed escapism. Lastly, chef Tye Hall fixes up a superb dish. Each of us has talents and gifts that help to make the world a safe space for all. Let's start planning what that vision looks like today. Thank you for supporting our magazine. You get a new look when you have SoulVision.

> "I look at my peers and the generation behind me and wonder what the future will be like for us."

NOVEMBER 2020

"What side of history will you be on?"

If you have not read Caste by Isabel Wilkerson (winner of the Pulitzer Prize for The Warmth of Other Suns) you should. This book also will win major book awards. It succinctly and objectively lays out the origins of our discontents. You probably won't be shocked to learn that Nazi Germany studied the American system to establish the diabolical regime that attempted to exterminate Jews. The book makes it clear why racists fly confederate flags and Nazi iconography almost interchangeably. The question presented is which side of history we will choose to be on, especially our white Brothers and Sisters who U.S. racists are trying to manipulate via fear tactics.

I believe the good people outnumber the bad. What I am not sure of is whether or not fear is more compelling than hope. It was love and hope that got us all through some dark days, so I choose love and hope.

If you really believe in the dream of America, the choice of who to vote for this presidential election cycle is a simple one. If you are blinded by the dog-whistles of racism and bigotry, the choice will appear more difficult. Say what you will. When it came down to voting in 2016—7/10 white men and 6/10 white women voted for Trump. I pray that in 2020 you will vote your faith and values and not your fears. A vote for hatred, bias, lies, indecency and hucksterism is a vote driven by fear. It's the same craziness and hysterics that led to Nazi Germany.

What side of history will you be on? What America do our children deserve? What's kind of ironic is that DNA wise, we are 99 percent the same. If the oldest human bones are found in Africa, then we are all descendants of and connected to that continent. How we got here is through a series of astonishing events, many lies, too many deceptions and numerous atrocities. Where we go from here will be determined by the way we VOTE. I pray you vote reason over race. I pray you vote love over hate. I pray that you love the dream of "America" as much as you say you do.

In this issue of SoulVision Magazine, we feature the great Jeffrey Wright. His talent is undeniable. In our candid conversation with Jeffrey, he reveals his process and his passion for cinema. Creatives Kingsley Kobayashi and Nova Lorraine share some of their magic sauce with us. We also include a sneak peek at the upcoming documentary—Ali's Comeback by Art Jones—detailing the resurgence of the pugilist legend's first fight after being stripped of his heavyweight title in 1967 at the tender age of 25. We close out the issue with a champion of childhood literacy—Carylee Carrington, a new recipe for the soul by chef Jerome Grant, and words of wisdom from media mogul and legend Paula Madison. You get a new look when you have SoulVision! Thank you for reading and sharing.

DECEMBER 2020

"It's a blessing to know who you are and where you come from."

It's a blessing to know who you are and where you come from. I was blessed to know all of my grandparents and three out of four of my great grandparents. I had meals with all of them and they shared things they saw and things they hoped for. I hope I am at least a sliver of their dreams. I hope my work and the way I live does honor to their memories and brings smiles to those gone but still rooting for us from on high. I pray that when it is our time to pass the batons of life, we have lived so well that our blueprint for justice, humanity and righteousness allows our children's children's children to step with alacrity into their purpose.

In this issue of SVM, we remember 2020. It was a tough year. We saw one of the worst global pandemics in history and the largest civil unrest in our nation's history. We closed the year with an election and the people elected a new President of the United States – Joe Biden – and the first woman in history – Kamala Harris – to be his Vice President. The outcome caused people to dance in the streets all over the world. Looking back, I'm glad we made it through 2020, and I am excited that we have the opportunity to go forward with leaders who are kind. In this issue of SVM, we review 2020 and highlight the best of SoulVision Magazine. Stay safe, happy holidays and see you next year!

> "Looking back, I'm glad we made it through 2020, and I am excited that we have the opportunity to go forward with leaders who are kind."

JANUARY 2021

"2020 was tough, but we woke up this morning in 2021. That's the GIFT."

My family did not take an exotic trip last year and that's OK. 2020 was tough, but we woke up this morning in 2021. That's the GIFT. Our Nation is getting everyone ready for a promising COVID-19 vaccine, and we are preparing to receive a new president and the first-ever woman vice president. It's a new day. Congratulations to President-elect Joe Biden and Vice President-elect Kamala Harris. It's official with inauguration festivities happening in the coming weeks. I had hoped that I would not lose any friends during this past election. Well, I did. I realized that some childhood acquaintances may never have been true friends? A friend has your back. They stay in touch. They clap when you win and help you through your struggles. They pray for you. They are honest with you, and together you strive to discover the blessings in life that you can both enjoy together. The people I lost after the 2020 Presidential election were none of those things. True, I knew them from elementary and high school and may have won some games with them as teammates, but they were never really my friends when it mattered. This realization puts the losses of 2020 in perspective for me. It actually lessened my burdens. Additionally, I was reminded that everyone you interact with will not be with you for all of your journey. Bigotry and hysteria are real and it's not my job (or yours) to fix that in everyone we meet. I decided to unsubscribe from toxic people. I wish everyone I've had to let go well, and I have resolved that my go-forward world is invite-only; reserved for my true family and friends.

So let's kickstart the energy in 2021. As one of my favorite motivational speakers – Lisa Nichols – reminds us, "put some extra on our ordinary . . . to get extraordinary!" This issue of SoulVision features the colorful, beautiful and healing art of Mr. Leroy Campbell. We also highlight the images of Lili Lathan and Heidi Abbott, two shutterbugs to watch. We close out the issue with a special story on the first African-American fountain designer in the US – Ms. Traer Price, an uplifting story on caring for our mental health, a first-time guest columnist story from Allyson Edge at Hampton University, and the presidential wisdom of none other than Barack Obama in our Legends section. You get a new look when you have SoulVision. Enjoy!

> "I wish everyone I've had to let go well, and I have resolved that my go-forward world is invite-only; reserved for my true family and friends."

FEBRUARY 2021

"[Our children] deserve a chance to live their best lives full of truth and the opportunity to be better."

This Nation of ours . . . a history lesson. Each time there is a rumbling at the core of our America, 3 major shifts can often be identified as the country is reimagined: 1) by 1868 after a bloody civil war – the Nation transformed with the 13th, 14th, and 15th Amendments to the US Constitution; 2) by 1968 after a pioneering Civil Rights movement – the Nation transformed with the Civil Rights Act, the Voting Rights Act and the Fair Housing Act; and 3) by 2021 after the largest protests in the history of our nation (over 23M after the killing of George Floyd) – once again (as of 3:49 AM on Jan. 7th) our Nation has transformed, handing the White House, the House, and the Senate to Democrats led by a white man and a black and Asian woman. What's more, it was the people and the VOTE that made this (AND ALL THE OTHER TRANSFORMATIONS) possible. The power is in the [people] to elect, not the [position] of President. It is ironic that in Georgia, a state where the KKK was founded, the people would elect a man of African descent and a man of Jewish descent to replace well funded white candidates who were on the wrong side of history. It is even more ironic because the same "Deep South" triumvirate of states, who were among the leaders of succession from the US invoking the Civil War (e.g., Georgia, Alabama, and Mississippi), in which two Jewish men and one African American man were murdered for trying to register people to vote decades earlier. Let that sink in. These transitions often cost precious lives. There is blood on the hands of the cowards and insurgents who would rather storm the US Capitol or suppress votes of fellow citizens with whom they disagree than to have a Nation that is actually governed by the people who make America a free democracy.

Now we have to take these great shifts in political tides and the knowledge that hate is too big a burden for our fragile Nation into account as we try to heal the country and govern with decency, empathy, and love. We must continue to fight the pandemic, improve our economy, and protect our planet from the damage humans have caused to it. Last, remember these hard-fought wins are not only for the good of America and a free world, they are for our children. They deserve a chance to live their best lives full of truth and the opportunity to be better. I pray that the age of the bigots and fools in charge is behind US? May God bless America. This issue of SoulVision features a cover story on the immeasurably talented Harry Lennix. In our cover story, Harry reveals his plans to build the "black version of the Lincoln Center for the Performing Arts" on the South Side of Chicago. Next, the creatives behind The Spot share their inspiration for building a community friendly space in Richmond. Ashish Manchanda discusses The Global Ikon, the first-ever global English music reality show. We also feature stories on rising Nigerian filmmaker Regina Udalor, hip-hop aficionado Alvin Glymph, a comfort food recipe from chef 'Ma' Michelle Wilson, and a contributing story from Hampton University student Drew Miles. Finally, we close out the issue with a tribute to the late great playwright Steve Carter from contributing writer Clyde Santana. You get a new look when you have SoulVision!

"Now we have to take these great shifts in political tides and the knowledge that hate is too big a burden for our fragile Nation into account as we try to heal the country and govern with decency, empathy, and love."

MARCH 2021

| "It's time to take back cool."

It's time to take back cool. When I grew up, I played basketball and was given a pass by the "cool kids" who could not beat me in the gym. I was labeled "different" as I pushed to get my studies done and play ball. I also was nice with karate thanks to my cousin Toni Lee. My Mom and Dad were respected teachers and leaders in the community. Showing up, paying bills, taking care of your family and going to a place of worship on Sunday was also cool back then. It was what we did in my world. Somehow I feel like we let cool slip into the hands of the hoodlums. Nowadays, you are only deemed tough or cool if you look like you can beat people up or you act like a fool in the face of authority. That's crazy! Standards are important. The baddest person at the club is not the one who can do the best twerk or breakdance, it's the person who can hold down that 9 to 5 the next morning. The cool person is the one who has a bank account with something in it besides hope. The baddest people in the room are the people who, in spite of all the obstacles working against them, get up each day and go out to face the world for their families. They make their house a home. That's what's up! That's cool. It's time to take back cool. Accordingly, in this issue celebrating powerful women, we highlight the incomparable Vernā Myers who's making diversity and inclusion a part of the culture at Netflix. We showcase creatives and designers Holly Byrd Miller, Robin Farmer, Sandrine Plante, and Benita Adams. In our Legends section, we celebrate the historical importance of Vice President Kamala Harris. All powerful women who know their worth and who are taking charge of their stories. Last, we close with Girls For A Change and a new dish from award-winning chef Katherine Thompson. Help us to celebrate the women who make the world go around. You get a new look when you have SoulVision!

> "The baddest person at the club is not the one who can do the best twerk or breakdance, it's the person who can hold down that 9 to 5 the next morning."

"Showing up is half the battle."

Showing up is half the battle. Don't just do it for you though. Include those who are up next. As a leader, you are in the pole position. You are the pace car. Leaders do not need to wait around for accolades, permission or inspiration. While all these things can help, leaders must do what is required to go forward when it's time to do something. We all get to choose how much energy we are willing to put into what we say we believe in. Leaders often have to do what others don't to achieve what others won't. In this issue, we take a leap forward with leaders, innovators and influencers who have found their gifts and who are using those gifts to change lives. Our April issue showcases the acting brilliance of Deborah Joy Winans, the educational excellence of Dr. Walter Milton Jr. and Joel Freeman with Black History 365, and the artistic genius of Baxter Perkinson Jr. We also chat with Rita Cohen, Page Turners and Michael "Boogie" Pinckney. Last, we light up the kitchen with chef JJ Johnson and salute the late great Vernon Jordan. Thank you for supporting excellence. You get a new look when you have SoulVision.

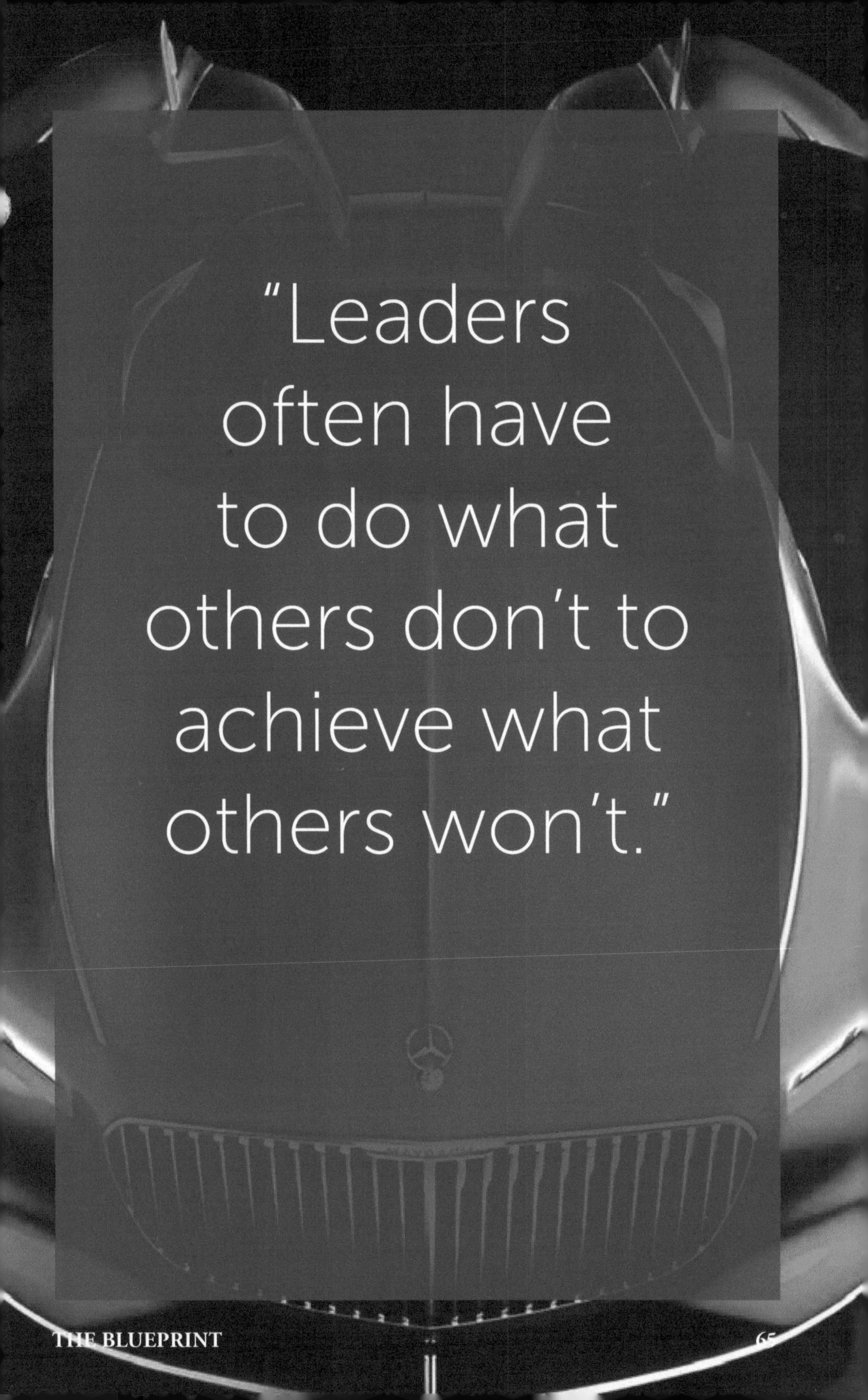

"Leaders
often have
to do what
others don't to
achieve what
others won't."

MAY 2021

I"Do it with love."

In the phenomenal blues song – "Baby What You Want Me To Do?" – the great bluesman Jimmy Reed sings about how his lady has him doing whatever she needs him to. It's classic blues, and there is a lot of truth in " . . . *you got me doin' what you want me to do.*" My Queen has me cooking and the practice has made me quite good at it, if I must say so myself. In fact, she talked me into my first celebrity cooking appearance just a few weeks ago. You can see the episode of *"Beyond the Plate RVA"* below. If you want this type of magic in your unions—be friends, share meals, enjoy each other's talents, and pray together. It's a simple formula to have your partner doing what you want them to do. What's more, when you do it with love, they usually reciprocate.

This issue of SoulVision Magazine is about people who are lifting us with inclusive fresh stories in books, narratives, and equations of time. We feature New York Times bestselling author David L. Robbins. David shares his latest work and what it takes to write convincingly about war and peace. We also spend some time with Nic King, who is empowering youth through the Legacy Cereal Company – the first black-owned cereal company in the U.S, and Bruce Nahin who is still making waves as a film producer. We travel into the world of unique international timepieces with the phenomenal master of horology Pietro Tomajer, founder of The Limited Edition, and catch up with RichWine RVA's creators Lance Lemon and Kristen Gardner Beal. Finally, we celebrate the genius of the late pioneering designer Jay Jaxon, share the latest from the Black Violin Foundation and showcase the culinary magic of chef Mike Lindsey.

"If you want this type of magic in your unions—be friends, share meals, enjoy each other's talents, and pray together."

You get a new look when you have SoulVision!

PHOTO BY HEIDI ABBOTT

JUNE 2021

"Remember the great blessing of **LIFE**."

BK FULTON

I'm not mad or angry at anyone today. Being pent up with a mask on my face for the last year and change was like being in a chrysalis for me. I've been working on me and trying to do everything that I can do to be a better version of myself. I've been reading, writing, cooking, thinking and praying that we would come out of this pandemic in a better place. My transformation included letting go of hate, anger, and any other weight that had become burdensome. I'm rocking with love and that makes me feel happy and light.

As we go into this summer with the pandemic mostly in our rear view mirrors, let's remember the great blessing of life that anyone reading this message gets to enjoy. We made it out of darkness and into a new light – today.

What will you do with your blessing?

In this issue of SoulVision Magazine, we examine diversity and inclusion from the perspective of an animation powerhouse – Lion Forge Animation. You will be surprised by the grit and insights from Lion Forge founders David Steward II and Carl Reed. We share the light of Tawn Williams, Ciarra Morris and Susan Brown. We also showcase the ingenuity of the young engineers at AirOn and go behind the scenes with a guest feature on the John F. Kennedy Center in Washington, D.C. In our Legends section, we acknowledge the impact and legacy of Robert Russa Moton, the second president of Tuskegee University. Last, chef Larry Carey brings the heat with a fantastic Honey Garlic Salmon & Shrimp with Asparagus recipe. Let's go all in with love!

You get a new look when you have SoulVision.

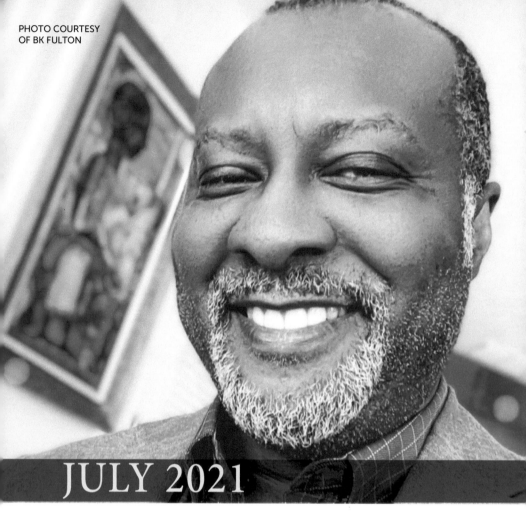

JULY 2021

"It's always been about the vote. Be sure to make yours matter."

Juneteenth is now officially a US Holiday! I'm happy about that, but it's not enough. The assault on our voting rights is real. Congress did not enact the law that would make the most difference for all Americans. Republicans at the national and state levels are working 24/7 to minimize the impact of voters who they don't think will support them. Super-partisan politics is a plague that we have to fight with what is right. Honoring the right to vote for all citizens should be a simple thing. However, trampling on the rights of others has been a consistent refrain in the American experiment. The best people in our nation must work diligently to keep the pressure on Congress and our State leaders. It's always been about the vote. Be sure to make yours matter.

In this issue, we talk to the phenomenal Hill Harper about his career and his Black Wall Street project. You'll be amazed by his family legacy and the way he is paying it forward. Mike Jones brings image magic with his stunning photography. Steve Glenn, DeShon Hardy, and Khadijah Smith remind us of the power of sharing our knowledge and talents with those from our neighborhoods. Our community feature highlights the Underground Kitchen's "UGK Community First" program, which addresses food insecurity in the Richmond Metro Region and Petersburg areas of Virginia. In our Legends section, we honor the great Sydney Poitier, and chef Steve Glenn brings the heat with a fantastic new recipe.

You get a new look when you have SoulVision

> "Honoring the right to vote for all citizens should be a simple thing."

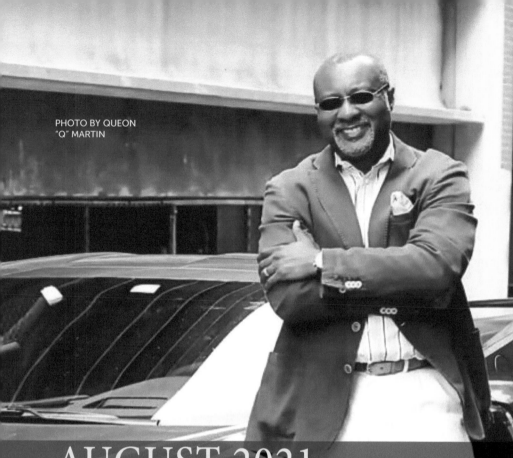

AUGUST 2021

"Do something great with your gifts."

I love history and most things mechanical. I also like well-made automobiles, watches, and pens. The C8 Stingray beside me was designed by none other than Ed Welburn — this month's SVM cover genius. Most people have no knowledge of the great contemporary design man. Prepare yourself for a treat. We go further in our *Legends* section by shining a light on C.R. Patterson. I had only a passing knowledge of this auto pioneer. His C.R. Patterson & Sons auto-manufacturing company sold hand-crafted cars in 1915 for under $700! Henry Ford sold Model-Ts for over $800 in 1908. Ford prices dropped to around $360 by 1916 as Henry Ford learned more about assembly work in "plants" from none other than George Washington Carver – the famous plant scientist from the glorious Tuskegee Institute. Ford visited with Dr. Carver frequently and even set up a lab for Dr. Carver to focus on his pioneering peanut and plant inventions. Some historians note that Ford in fact got the idea of the "assembly plant" from Carver. Ford is credited with bringing affordable automobiles to the masses. I wonder what might have happened if C.R. Patterson had received the financial backing and support afforded Mr. Ford? Think about it on your next drive and share his history with your kids. If C.R. can build cars in 1915, our kids can do anything by the grace of God . . . .

This issue of SVM is all about getting it done. As I mentioned earlier, our cover feature is on the great Ed Welburn. He spent four decades shaping the iconic output of General Motors and for most of his career was the highest-ranking person of color in the industry. We also highlight makers like Vontélle co-founders Tracy Vontélle Green and Nancey Harris, Melody Roscher, and Angela Jefferson whose poetry will lift your spirits. We close out with an inspirational story from the Urban League of Philadelphia and their amazing president and CEO Andrea Custis. Finally, we bring the heat with a lovely dish from chef Ida MaMusu who recently celebrated the opening of a larger restaurant space with extended hours. It's our time. Do something great with your gifts. You get a new look when you have SoulVision!

> "I wonder what might have happened if C.R. Patterson had received the financial backing and support afforded Mr. [Henry] Ford?"

"God is in the details. Make great art."

SEPTEMBER 2021

It was cool to find out that my 2021 Producers Guild of America (PGA) class includes the legendary Dolly Parton. She's one of my favs and now I get to call her my PGA classmate. How cool is that! When we started SoulVision Magazine, we set out to show the beauty and excellence in all of humanity. We continue to push forward, completely excited about the possibilities before us.

In this issue, we keep the magic going with a cover story on game theory wizards Mike and Josh Grier, the founders of

"When we started SoulVision Magazine, we set out to show the beauty and excellence in all of humanity."

Ember Lab, an independent animation, digital, and gaming studio. We catch up with filmmakers Tremayne Johnson and Mario Jackson, multi-hyphenates Keats and Chavon Hampton, and detail the craftsmanship of watch strap maker David Richards. We also highlight the important work of RPAA's Greater Richmond Wolf Trap program and give you a hearty dish from chef April Shepperson. Finally, we pay homage to one of the greatest NBA players of all time, the late Kobe Bryant.

God is in the details. Make great art.

THE BLUEPRINT

OCTOBER 2021

"The show must go on."

The show must go on. Life is a dynamic thing with natural ups and downs. We make most of the best parts of life happen in between by doing the work. In fact, as I've said here before, the win is in the work. This week a new monument to freedom went up in Richmond, Virginia. It's the first of its kind in the United States. In a moment of universal karma, just a few weeks ago, the last major confederate monument in Virginia came down. In fact, it was one of the largest Confederate monuments in the nation and the last of its kind in the former Capital of the Confederacy. Times change and we must continue to do the work to push our nation forward so that needed changes give hope to our children. They deserve every chance to be the best version of themselves. We set their best lives in motion by what we do today; each day.

In this issue of SoulVision Magazine, we celebrate the great showman Ron Simons. He is a force on Broadway and more importantly, he is a man on a mission. We also share with you stories on Swiss watchmaker Vincent Plomb's Vicenterra, talent manager Wink, and filmmaker Robert Nyerges. We also take a look at Ron Simons' Broadway play Thoughts of a Colored Man and give you a recipe from acclaimed food blogger Karelle Vignon-Vullierme. Finally, we highlight the educational and nonprofit work of the Treehouse Group and give appreciation to stage and silent film legend Bert Williams.

PHOTO COURTESY OF BK FULTON

"We must lift as we climb."

NOVEMBER 2021

We must lift as we climb. I'm amazed by the resilience of educators who pour into young lives so that one day we might become the best version of ourselves. It's really cool when you think about it. We are all an aggregate of our experiences. As we learn more, one of the rights of passage into adulthood requires that we give more. Since teaching is a form of giving, I'm focusing this month's note on teaching more and not just in the *each one teach one sense . . . ,* but in the each one teach as many as you can sense. You see, we all can do something to make the world better. It is my core belief that anyone can teach. There is something special about each of us. And it is a supreme gift to give back; to pour into future generations so that this thing called humanity advances. My parents are educators. I started my professional career as an instructor in the Bronx, NY.

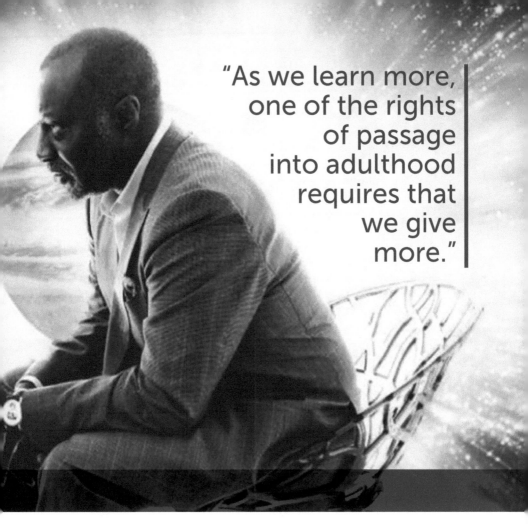

"As we learn more, one of the rights of passage into adulthood requires that we give more."

Today, through our networks, films, and this magazine, we carry forward the tradition of caring and sharing through teaching others.

Accordingly, in this issue of SoulVision Magazine, we highlight the brilliance and wisdom of Academy COO Christine Simmons, learn how to succeed in our second act with Benita Adams, and witness the power of learning from multi-hyphenate Tanya Boucicaut. We also learn about the craftsmanship behind Karen Cooper's smoking wands, get a BBQ-ready recipe from Brenda L. Thomas and take a look at her cookbook Sayin' A Taste. Finally, we share the inspirational story behind entrepreneur and model Kathare Mundit's African Benefit Society nonprofit, and celebrate the legacy of Hattie McDaniel.

THE BLUEPRINT

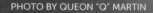

"Collaboration is essential to living out the dreams that constantly take up space in our heads."

DECEMBER 2021

Collaboration is essential to living out the dreams that constantly take up space in our heads. We all live in a community and have the opportunity to collaborate with our neighbors. Successful collaboration requires a mutual sense of respect. It requires an understanding of one's own belief in their creativity. It requires the artist to make a decision and not to be afraid to go with what they feel in their spirit. A great artist calls on friends and strangers alike to talk out their ideas, fully formed or not. They then will go into solitude and create. But when that artist emerges from solitude, they must show what they created to the world. They must count on the support of these same friends and strangers to reap the fruits of their labor.

For the last three years, SoulVision Magazine has supported the work of creatives and visionaries. Our cover stories from this year can tell us a thing or two about working together. Broadway producer Ron Simons works with playwrights, directors, producers, and actors to create stage plays that are humorous, memorable, and heartwarming. Author David L. Robbins leads writing workshops with veterans healing from the psychological wounds of war. The Academy COO Christine Simmons works with film industry tastemakers, artists, and executives to make a more inclusive and diverse motion picture industry. Ember Lab co-founders Mike and Josh Grier called on a team of video game designers and developers to create the fantastical world of *Kena: Bridge of Spirits.*

Creating a magazine is collaborative work. In the world of publishing, we count on writers, editors, photographers, videographers, graphic designers, advertisers and other creatives to create a magazine that is worth reading and sharing. Thank you for sticking with us for another year. We look forward to seeing you in 2022. Happy holidays!

"A great artist calls on friends and strangers alike to talk out their ideas, fully formed or not."

JANUARY 2022

I "Be there for others."

I recently read about a little girl who could not afford running sneakers for her school's track meet, so she taped her feet and drew Nike logos on the tape. She went on to win gold in the 400 metres, 800 metres and the 1500 metres. That is an example of faith and action converging for miraculous outcomes. Just like the little girl, we make things happen in life because we put in the work. Whether it's running a race on a track or running the race of life, anyone can serve because any of us can become the best version of ourselves. Be there for others; it comes back tenfold. In fact, God will pour you out a blessing that you can hardly receive. We win not because we are great. We win because God is great.

In this month's issue of SoulVision Magazine we continue our pursuit of human excellence with a feature on jazz prodigy and multi-instrumentalist Matthew Whitaker. We also share shorts on entrepreneur Javona Braxton, and Ben Tankard, the father of Gospel Jazz. In this month's issue, we learn more about and get a recipe from Virginia Tech student Tahjere Lewis, chat with Dr. Jade Ranger about her first published book, and highlight the Boys Home of Virginia's Playground Project. Finally, we honor celebrated sociologist and the eighth president of Morgan State University, Dr. Andrew Billingsley.

My prayer for each of us is that we become the best version of ourselves; if not for us, for our children. Bring all of you into 2022.

> "We win not because we are great.
>
> We win because God is great."

FEBRUARY 2022

I "Each day is a gift."

Each day is a gift. What we do with that gift is our gift back to humanity. We all are praying that 2022 is better than 2021. It's natural to hope for the best in every new year. What I think is also natural is that we each get to have the world we are willing to work for. I no longer pray that I will find life's joys as others validate my expressions. I now pray that God continues to lift me and give me the health and strength to keep doing what is right. I make this my prayer because I have found that as long as I do what is right, I don't have to find joy; joy finds me. In other words, become a pace car of life.

Be the example of integrity; the example of God's grace and mercy; the example of love and faith in action. This is where I find myself halfway through my journey. In this issue of SoulVision Magazine, we introduce you to people whose excellence has made them the pace cars of humanity. They are busy doing the work and by doing so, they give love a chance.

Our cover story features Grammy Award-winning producer and engineer Commissioner Gordon Williams. We also share shorts on Dr. Princess Chinyere Halliday, artist M. Sani, and creative Dave Ortiz's Our/New York. We also take a look at Michelle Coles' debut novel and share with you a savory recipe from chef Tiara Smith. Finally, we highlight the nonprofit Girls on the Run of Greater Richmond and honor the one and only Betty White. You get a new look when you have SoulVision!

> "I have found that as long as I do what is right, I don't have to find joy; joy finds me."

MARCH 2022

| "We've come a long way."

While we still have work to do, I believe we have to recognize
the progress we've made since our beginnings in this land some
400 years ago. I was reminded of this truth during my recent
visit to Jackson, Mississippi for the World Premiere of our latest
film A Day to Die featuring Bruce Willis, Leon, Kevin Dillon, and
Frank Grillo. During our trip we visited the Mississippi Civil
Rights Museum before going on a tour of our Jackson-based
studio. As fate would have it, Mr. Hezekiah Watkins was working
at the museum during our visit. You may not know his name, but
I hope you have heard of the "Freedom Riders." At only
13 when he was arrested, Hezekiah was the youngest of the
Freedom Riders taken to death row at the infamous Parchman
Prison. He was only out that day to see what all the fuss was
about in downtown Jackson, Mississippi. He had no idea that he
would be arrested and taken directly to prison where he would
be beaten and brutalized by adult inmates on death row for
murder and other violent crimes. This was 1961; clearly within
our lifetimes. Mr. Watkins was steadfast in his resolve that
while he did not choose his moment in history, he helped
to clear the way for integrated bus riding for all passengers
no matter what ethnicity. It was a victory achieved at great

cost. I shared with Hezekiah that because of his sacrifice, our production team was able to film a real Hollywood shoot-em up with explosions and helicopters just blocks from where Hezekiah was arrested. The African American Mayor, local businessmen and women, college students, and locals from around Mississippi were on hand to celebrate the completion of our film. We've come a long way.

In this issue of SoulVision Magazine we celebrate Women's History Month by highlighting the work of media pioneer Daphne Maxwell Reid. She has been making a way out of no way in a career spanning 43 years. We also share with you stories on emerging designer, model, and bodybuilder Jordan Clark, take a look at A Day to Die, and witness NY Racing Team make NASCAR history with the Grambling State University #44 car. This month we also share with you a recipe from Chef Moe and highlight fem-treneur Jean Drummond's innovative healthcare consulting firm, HCDI. Finally, we appreciate the eclectic and captivating art of the Black American Artists Alliance of Richmond and honor one of America's most celebrated poets, Dr. Maya Angelou. You get a new look when you have SoulVision!

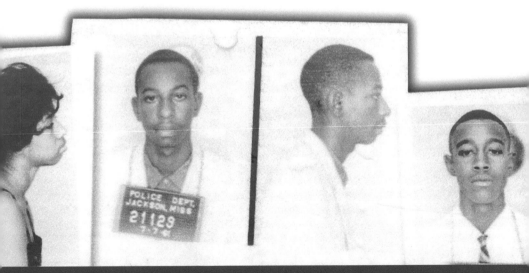

HEZEKIAH WATKINS WAS A THIRTEEN-YEAR-OLD STUDENT AT ROWAN JUNIOR HIGH WHEN HE WAS ARRESTED AT THE GREYHOUND BUS STATION ON JULY 7. **HE WAS THE YOUNGEST OF THE FREEDOM RIDERS.**

GREYHOUND BUS STATION

On May 28, 1961, a Greyhound bus with nine Freedom Riders aboard arrived here, the third group of Riders into Jackson. The first two came on Trailways buses May 24. That summer 329 people were arrested in Jackson for integrating public transportation facilities. Convicted on "breach of peace" and jailed, most refused bail and were sent to the state penitentiary. Their protest worked. In September 1961, the federal government mandated that segregation in interstate transportation end.

PLACED DURING THE 50TH ANNIVERSARY OF THE FREEDOM RIDES-1961-2011

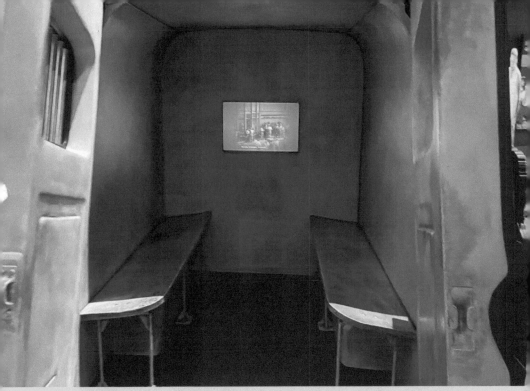

WHEN FREEDOM RIDERS GOT OFF THE GREYHOUND BUS, THE LOCAL POLICE PUT THEM INTO THE PADDY WAGON

"While we still have work to do, I believe we have to recognize the progress we've made since our beginnings in this land some 400 years ago."

THE BLUEPRINT

APRIL 2022

> "I am reminded that in the face of evil or wrongdoing the brave must not despair."

Springtime is here. The cherry blossoms in Washington, DC are in bloom. The pandemic is fading away. Around the world people are excited about returning to something that feels like normal. I'm excited too, although I am still very worried about what is happening in Ukraine. Modern technology and media have made the world a much smaller place to traverse. We can flip on any news channel and be transported to events thousands of miles away. What's more, common citizens through blogs, drones, and other Internet applications are setting up virtual desks to report on what's happening in their corner of the planet. Many days, the news brings hope like the little Ukrainian girl singing for her homeland. On other days the news is grim like the loss of a mother and child who were the innocent victims of Russian bombings on their peaceful nation. I am reminded that in the face of evil or wrongdoing the brave must not despair. The courageous must stand up and speak truth to power. We hope this issue of SoulVision Magazine will inspire you to be courageous.

We feature the pioneering plastic surgeon – Dr. Michael Jones – who has invented a scar removal surgery with over 98% effectiveness. In this month's issue, we also share with you stories on musical artists Karuna Shinsho, ONE, and Sidney Outlaw, and take a look at Emblem Olive's high-quality products. Finally, we share with you a recipe from the viral Monica Singh, show the empowering work of Pretty Purposed, and celebrate the legacy of Dr. John A. Kenney, Sr. You get a new look when you have SoulVision!

> "Modern technology and media have made the world a much smaller place to traverse."

MAY 2022

"When you inspire someone, you ignite a positive future."

I've learned through many trials and tribulations that we can manifest greatness by lifting each other. I found my way to success by reading about the wins of my ancestors. Knowing that they made a way out of no way inspired me. Their stories gave me a blueprint for living, learning and giving. It's as if their love poured over the fires of my failures and was the catalyst for my phoenix to arise from the ashes. I owe so much to people I've never met. What I believe they would want us all to do is to pay their gifts forward for future generations. That is the power of inspiration. It's eternal. It's a gift that keeps on giving. When you inspire someone, you ignite a positive future. Our world deserves a positive future. The good news is that we already possess everything required to be great. It starts with inspiration.

In this issue of SoulVision Magazine, we hope to inspire you with the phenomenal work of Leon, an actor's actor. We also share with you stories on iWoman TV founder Cathleen Trigg-Jones, musician extraordinaire Tom E Morrison, audio engineer Matt Treacy, and photographer Chris McGee. Finally, we give you a fun recipe from Chef Jacoby Ponder, take a look at the important educational work of Partnership for the Future, and honor the legacy of singer, actor, and activist Paul Robeson.

"I found my way to success by reading about the wins of my ancestors."

JUNE 2022

"Our children are our most important resource."

Our children are our most important resource. They are the future. We can not continue to lose our babies to senseless gun violence. I am a veteran and believe in responsible ownership of firearms. Even so, I also believe in sensible rules to govern who can own them, what type can be owned by civilians, and under what conditions they can be concealed. People who are not well are not ready for gun ownership. People who are violent are not ready for gun ownership. People who are not trained are not ready for gun ownership. I'm willing to balance my second amendment rights with community safety because I love our nation and the youth who must take us forward. We've given this issue enough lip service. Fully 80% of the nation believes in some form of rational gun control. We must do the hard work to find common ground if we want to end the increasing trend of violent homicides in the US. Why do we have to do this you might ask? We have to do it for our children. I am a parent, and like any loving parent I want my children to grow up to be what God has made them to be.

These are my boys. I am smiling because they make me happy. I am proud of them. I love them more than they will ever know. I want them to grow up knowing that Mommy and Daddy did all they knew how to do to raise them the right way. These are MY boys. Soon they will be men and it will be their charge to raise their sons (and daughters) to be all that the Lord has blessed them to be. I don't want them to become a statistic. I want them to be inspired by what good people did to keep them safe.
In this issue of SoulVision Magazine we keep the community uplift going by sharing the inspiring story of Ms. Sophia A. Nelson and her pioneering journalism that asks us to look deeper as we solve the most pressing issues facing our society. We also share with you stories on lawyer and novelist Leslie T. Thornton, artist Karen Terry, and singer and actress Beverly Ann Booker. We also give you a look at chef Jacoby Ponder's new cooking class. Finally, we share a traditional recipe from chef Sharde' Dantzler, support the fundraising goal of Girls For A Change and honor the legacy of Tusla lawyer and author, the late B.C. Franklin.

"We must do the hard work to find common ground if we want to end the increasing trend of violent homicides in the US."

COMMUNITY

"Our power lies in community."

This will be short and brief: The U.S. Supreme Court overturning Roe v. Wade is shameful. But this shouldn't be a moment to panic. This is a moment to organize. This is a moment to look to our neighbors and community for support. Reproductive choice is freedom. Reproductive choice is economic security and opportunity. We all can do our part by donating to and giving your time to your local abortion fund, participating in a local protest, calling or emailing your representative in the Senate and House and letting your voice be heard. This is not meant to be an exhaustive list, but when we come together, the powers that be are forced to listen. As creatives and visionaries, we must also work together to make society a better place.

We must use our art and platforms to speak about injustices wherever they are and rally our audiences to take direct action, whenever they can. Whether we like to admit it or not, politics are personal.

[participation + relationships + empathy]

The creatives and visionaries featured in this month's issue are doing their part. Our cover story, innovative advocate and multimedia host Chris Denson's most recent episode of Work in Progress speaks about the importance of women's sexual health. Relationship expert Love McPherson is teaching couples how to strengthen their love. Creative artist Duane Doku is working directly with and speaking out on mental health through fashion. Susan Smallwood is making luxury more inclusive. Author and teacher Nia Nicole is using her book sales to fund her nonprofit for our youth. Boys Home of Virginia is creating a space for boys to be themselves. Chef Jacoby Ponder is bringing families back together. The words of late feminist and intellectual bell hooks inspire us to make a community that is inclusive, fair, and loving. What kind of world do you want to live in? Our power lies in community.

"This is a moment to look to our neighbors and community for support."

"Don't judge a book by its cover."

AUGUST 2022

Recently I was reminded of the old adage ". . . don't judge a book by its cover." Those words are as true now as they have ever been. I thought of the axiom while watching the 2022 release of Elvis. From the beginning to the end I enjoyed the film and was shocked by some of the revelations. I did not appreciate that he grew up in a Black community. I did not appreciate that he learned some of his moves in the Black church, preferred African American back up singers, loved the blues, and was close with Black music greats like BB King. When I was in college, "Fight The Power," a song by the rap group Public Enemy set the table for my judging Elvis unfairly. The line from the song that would become a social justice anthem went like this – "Elvis, was a hero to most, but he never meant s*#@ to me; straight out racist, the sucker was simple and plain, mother-f*#* him and John Wayne." I still remember the lines and dancing to the song; ostensibly accepting the lyrics of Chuck-D and Public Enemy word for word without any question. After seeing the film, I decided to do a little research. What I found has caused me to change my opinion of Elvis. First, even Chuck-D backed away from the original lyrics. He still said that Elvis appropriated Black music and benefited from it in a way that Black artists could not at the time. I don't have a quarrel with that notion. It was 1950s America and appropriation of our talents was commonplace.

Even so, Elvis was a bridge between Black music and white culture. That too is undeniable. What I also learned was that the reasons people thought Elvis was racist were largely inflated or made up. This came from the chief editor of the then-popular Jet Magazine, the backup singers for Elvis, the pastor of the Black church where Elvis learned some of his signature moves, and the likes of BB King. Who am I to refute these contemporaneous accounts of a man that I did not know? In fact, I grew up watching his movies and enjoyed most of them. I did not fall out with Elvis until I heard that one song during my college days. Now I am older and wiser and when I look at the facts, I respect Elvis for the person he was and appreciate that he befriended many people that I respect throughout his career. We have to be the change we seek and if we want people to see our community differently, we have to be active participants in how we interact with and judge others.

In this issue, we continue to share excellence and truth by bringing the best from all communities. Our cover story this month is NBA Vice President and Assistant General Counsel Tatia L. Williams. Also in this month's issue, we share with you the inspirational story of real estate leader Nancy E. Johnson, take a look at the inspirations behind the work of rising singer/songwriter Trae Taylor, rising filmmaker Alyssa Brayboy, and former NFL player and artist Richard Clebert. Finally, we share with you the perfect summertime recipe from chef Kyle Taylor, highlight the Presidential Precinct's Mandela Washington Fellowship program, and celebrate the legacy of Maggie L. Walker.

"We have to be the change we seek and if we want people to see our community differently,

MAGGIE L. WALKER

we have to be active
participants in how we
interact with and
judge others."

"Truth in obscurity is more precious than fame based on falsehoods."

SEPTEMBER 2022

Truth in obscurity is more precious than fame based on falsehoods. We live in a time in which everyone seems to question everything and they will say anything for their 15 minutes of fame. While some questioning of authority is healthy in a democracy, it's a problem when people en masse believe their internet research is more accurate than established news outlets, bonafide experts and government agencies that are duty bound to report with transparency. Normal has shifted. Our political discourse has become too jaded and mean-spirited. In this climate of uncertainty, we have to push reset and get back to truth as a starting point. A divided nation is a weaker nation. Our enemies know this and will use every device to misinform our communities. Accordingly, we must allow truth to set us free. We must lean into helping our neighbors and lifting our nation . . . together.

In this issue of SoulVision Magazine, we discuss the metaverse and the future of education with entrepreneur Marcus Shingles. Next, we explore the artistry of author and writer B.C. FaJohn, rising filmmaker Myles Brown, and engraver David Harris. Also in this month's issue, we update you on chef Kyle Taylor's new restaurant and share a delicious and healthy recipe from chef Andre Carthen. Finally, we highlight the valuable work of the National Education Equity Lab, and celebrate the legacy of Nichelle Nichols. You get a new look when you have SoulVision!

"We must lean into helping our neighbors and lifting our nation . . . together."

LOVE Is the Secret Ingredient

OCTOBER 2022

"I hope when people read our magazine or take in our shows or films they feel the love that we put into the work."

"I hope when people read our magazine or take in our shows or films they feel the love that we put into the work." It has been seven years since BK Fulton retired from his executive position in corporate America and began laying the foundation for the media and investment company Soulidifly Productions, officially established in 2017. As he has eloquently stated in various interviews throughout the years, "I spent the first fifty years of my life doing what I was trained to do, now I am doing what I was made to do."

In the last year, Soulidifly has made an impact on Broadway. Its first investment in Broadway was *Thoughts of a Colored Man*, a powerful story of seven Black men and their perspectives on what it means to be Black men in the 21st century. It garnered critical acclaim, winning a GLAAD award for Outstanding Broadway Production and eligibility for a Tony. *Thoughts of a Colored Man*'s run was successful but due to covid restrictions, the play was forced to close prematurely. It was the number one new show on Broadway during its two month run. This fall, Soulidifly is back on Broadway with August Wilson's Pulitzer Prize-winning play *The Piano Lesson*, directed by LaTanya Richardson Jackson and starring Samuel L. Jackson, John David Washington, and Danielle Brooks. *The Piano Lesson* tells the story of the Charles family and their struggle to preserve their family legacy.

The company's award-winning films helped BK earn membership in the prestigious Producers Guild of America on his first attempt. This year, Soulidlfiy has already had several major successes. Soulidifly's latest release, *A Day to Die*, was Bruce Willis' last film and has garnered a newfound appreciation for the acting chops of both Bruce and his co-star Leon. Soulidifly's investment in MoviePass 2.0 had over 775,000 sign-ups to its beta launch waitlist. Looking ahead to next year, BK's top priority is to double down on the company's investments including a blockbuster cast for *The Kill Room* with Samuel L. Jackson and Uma Thurman. For this interview, BK spoke with the co-founding editor of SoulVision Magazine, Nicholas Powell, about the future of Soulidifly Productions, the intentions behind the work, and his own personal reflections on life and success.

THIS YEAR MARKS THE FIFTH ANNIVERSARY OF SOULIDIFLY PRODUCTIONS. WHAT VALUABLE LESSONS HAVE YOU LEARNED IN THOSE FIVE YEARS?

In the last five years, I've learned that consistency is critical to business success. Typically you see a 3-5 year arch in profitability for startups as they develop their footing. Part of our growth period was hit hard by a global pandemic that could have potentially wiped out years of effort. People weren't going to the theaters, but fortunately we had online and digital properties that helped us weather the storm.

Because we started our business a few years before the pandemic, we were in a better position than other production companies that started later than we did. I think we had the blessing of good timing on our side. We were able to stay consistent and accordingly emerged on the backend of the pandemic as a stronger company by demonstrating high production values and showing modest revenue. I am grateful we were able to keep our team together.

"Our industry has become prolific at producing our tragedies. We have to be equally prolific about our triumphs too."

LOOKING TOWARDS THE FUTURE, ARE THERE ANY STORIES YOU WOULD LIKE TO PRODUCE?

I would love to produce the Chevalier de Saint-Georges story. He was a great Black composer from the 1700s. This year at the Jackson Film Festival, we launched the Soulidifly Productions Blueprint Script & Media Prize, which awards up to $10,000 for the best script on Saint-Georges or Lewis Latimer, the famed scientist who helped Edison create the electric lightbulb. I also hope we get backing for our project *Final Four: The Miracle Season* about Coach V (Jim Valvano) and the 1983 NC State Wolfpack's championship run. We also are pitching *Asira Awakens*, Malik Yoba's directorial debut. I would love to see our collaboration with Lion Forge Animation on the *Mr. Business* animated series show up at a major streaming studio like Disney+, Netflix, Amazon, Hulu, BET+ or Apple TV.

There is a popular Black history book that we may be able to wrap some stage magic around, and we are in talks to produce a Nina Simone play on Broadway that celebrates her talent and the many people she influenced.

There are a few documentaries I would like to produce—one in the civil rights space, one that highlights our impact on car racing, and another about scientific discovery and invention—all centering around people of color. These are the stories that are not getting told. We need to tell these stories. It is not only good for children who are so-called underrepresented minorities, but it is also good for everyone. Our industry has become prolific at producing our tragedies. We have to be equally prolific about our triumphs too.

When I look at textbooks, I think about my own training and journey. In my youth, I was not aware of any of the heroes and sheroes who happened to look like me. I think if I had been more aware, I would have gone into college with a different belief in myself. I would have done better in high school. I would have done better, period, because I wouldn't have assumed that all of the great things I saw in the world were not for or from people like me. I lost a few years not including myself in the achievement narrative of humanity. Good stories and receiving better information helps to expand minds. Stories of success fueled my rise in corporate America and sparked this half of my journey.

RECENTLY, SOULIDIFLY INVESTED IN AUGUST WILSON'S THE PIANO LESSON, STARRING SAMUEL L. JACKSON, JOHN DAVID WASHINGTON, AND DANIELLE BROOKS. WHAT INSPIRED YOU TO BE A PART OF THIS PRODUCTION?

August Wilson is one of my favorites. He is Broadway royalty. There is an unreleased story about early August Wilson that I would love to see come to life. I have a friend who is a former corporate executive like myself who wrote a story about her mom who took care of August and became connected with him for a while. This was before August Wilson was the man he would become. He sat in her diner creating what would become some of his greatest work while she nourished him with her food and love. It is a beautiful love story that took place at the dawn of the civil rights movement. It's him writing his stories of common folk and their trials and tribulations. This was an ordinary sister in a diner who saw a brother struggling and helped him to work it out. He wrote love letters to her and her daughter has the letters Wilson wrote to her mother. These heartfelt letters are beautiful and all end with "From August, With Love."

"Much like earning a college degree, the rewards in the film and media business are often delayed."

BEAUTIFUL. WHEN YOU LOOK AT YOUR WORK THUS FAR, WHAT IS THE MESSAGE YOU WANT PEOPLE TO GET FROM YOUR WORK?

As I think about our magazine and the work we do in our community, love is at the center. There is a brilliant gentleman I met recently on Martha's Vineyard. His name is Richard Hunt, a preeminent African American sculptor of our time. He was the first African American sculptor to have an exhibit at MoMA in New York. I found out he had a sculpture in my community in Newport News, Virginia, where I was baptized as a kid. This blew my mind! He is now a cherished friend.

Not enough people know his story. Now in his 80s, Richard Hunt is a national treasure. I would love for stories about people like Richard to see the light of day. Richard is someone who cares so much for his fellow man that his life's work of sculpture is about helping human beings to appreciate each other. There is a lot of love in that sentiment and I hope when people read our magazine or take in our shows or films, they feel the love that we put into the work.

WHAT ADVICE WOULD YOU GIVE TO THE NEXT GENERATION OF FILMMAKERS?

The young talent I like to work with have a healthy respect for the past but are looking toward the future. I hope they don't quit too easily when they encounter obstacles because in this business, there are a lot of disappointments. People sometimes don't do what they say they are going to do. Some of the projects are expensive and if you don't have the capital, you can't quite create on the scale you may have hoped for. Tomorrow's media makers can't let these realities of the business discourage them from creating great art. I want young creatives to keep going.

We live in the real world and in the real world there are many compelling interests. Somebody likes painting. Somebody likes music. Somebody likes movies. In these spaces, our young people can achieve and exceed what prior generations have done. However, patience will be required.

I often find with young adults that they want all their wins right now and they want fame to happen really fast. Delayed gratification appears to be a punishment to them as opposed to the reward at the end of a long journey.

Much like earning a college degree, the rewards in the film and media business are often delayed. Not everybody gets an Oscar with their first movie. That rarely happens for any movie. If young creatives love this powerful medium however, they will have to crawl before they walk and walk before they run. As they build momentum, build skills, build their portfolios and build their network, then they will likely have more success and one day accept their Oscar, Emmy, Tony or Image award.

We are five years into this with two Broadway shows, 15 books, and 18 films that have been released or are in the works. We've learned a lot, won some awards and we are getting better. So I tell the next generation, don't give up; stay the course.

"There is a long road to success in this business and they should lean in and enjoy the ride."

WHAT'S UP NEXT?

We have a fun sci-fi project with Wes Miller called *Our Future's Past* that will release in the film festival circuit soon. *Freedom's Path* should be acquired or released in early 2023. *The Kill Room* also will come out in 2023. It's our largest project to-date. Uma Thurman and Samuel L. Jackson reunite in this art world-meets-underworld comedic thriller. Fans have not seen Sam and Uma together since the iconic Pulp Fiction. We will release a few more books next year including 2 novels. I'd like to bring back *Thoughts of a Colored Man* for travel shows and streaming. I almost forgot to mention our film with Kelly Rowland called 3 Mile Inn. It's a fun thriller we hope to start shooting this year or early next year. We are going to have a powerful cast co-starring alongside her. *A Day to Die* did well, so we are looking for actors of Bruce Willis' and Leon's caliber to join us in the fun. We are building a production studio in Mississippi that should be operational before the end of the year. The state provides a great tax credit and hopefully, other states will provide additional incentives as well. Finally, we are putting the finishing touches on MediaU.com. It's our online film school with real university credits and transcripts. We will train the next million media makers and help them build their careers.

A flexible and well-run media company can adjust quickly.

> "We know great stories. We know how to tell them and have assembled an expert team that can package them."

We will keep on doing what we are doing and amplify what works and cut what doesn't. Most of all, I hope to keep enjoying the process of making impactful art. Our fans deserve the very best we can offer.

NOVEMBER 2022

> **"I'm still learning, expanding, evolving and becoming a wiser new form."**

Over the past few days I have been reflecting on our ancestors and how so many people came together to make the world special. Recently I was able to spend a few hours with the great sculptor – Richard Hunt – and was moved by the way he told stories with metal and fire. His art forms have a way of dancing even though they are still objects. It's as if he is capturing an ever-fluid moment of creation, expansion, evolution, and new forms. This is our world. Spending some time with the great artist, his friends and others who care about his work – I'm now the self-appointed Vice Chairman of Richard's Fan Club (David Grain is the self-appointed Chairman, and Jon Ott is the actual President) – has inspired me to share a poem that I wrote when I was a younger man. I'm still learning, expanding, evolving and becoming a wiser new form.

Force Vitale

If not now! . . . when?

Do you feel the spirit rising in us?
. . . around us.

The Brothers are back!
New men.
Spiritual men.

Men who define themselves.
Men who do not buckle in the face of adversity.
Men who love their women.
Men who love their children.
Men who love their world.
Men who love themselves.

Like great rocks that rise out of solid ground
. . . we move forward unafraid.

I thank God almighty that I am alive
. . . to be a part of this movement.

It is no longer enough that we survive.
It is time to develop and prosper.

On the strength of your and my ancestors
. . . before we are through
. . . this world will be a better place.

In this issue of SoulVision Magazine, we profile Acadamy Award-winning costume designer Ruth E. Carter. Next, we highlight the work of Stylegasm's Jennifer Koch, Allez Watch Company's co-founder Ethan Evans, and Crewel and Unusual's creator Daniel Crawford. Also in this month's issue, we take a look at stylists Maria V. Williams and Angelique Michelle's new venture and a savory recipe from chef Martel Stone. Finally, we highlight the great literary work of critically acclaimed author Adriana Trigiani and Nancy Bolmeir Fisher's The Origin Project and pay homage to legendary fashion designer Willi Smith. You get a new look when you have SoulVision!

DECEMBER 2022

From left: Nicholas Powell (Co-founding Editor of SoulVision Magazine), BK Fulton (Founding Chairman, CEO of Soulidifly Productions), Queon "Q" Martin (Executive Vice President of Soulidifly Productions).

> "The world is made better when we choose to make it better."

Over the past four years we have worked hard to deliver excellence to you month after month. We hope you have enjoyed SoulVision Magazine. At this time, we have decided to suspend the monthly publication to focus on the film, stage and investment areas of our business. We have chosen to continue our practice of sharing motivational news and projects from time to time so you remain aware of what inspires us to do all things in a great way.

We began the year with 21-year-old jazz prodigy and multi-instrumentalist Matthew Whitaker and ended the year with a career-spanning profile of Academy Award-winning costume designer Ruth E. Carter. In between, we profiled entrepreneurs, actors, authors, and artists we felt would interest our readers. Throughout the years as we researched and interviewed visionaries from the past and present, we found ourselves not only empowered but moved to continue the good work in our personal and professional lives. Many of you have told us how our work has moved you as well. We thank you for your support throughout the years.

It has been our privilege to get to know the wonderful human beings who have been featured in SoulVision Magazine. The world is made better when we choose to make it better. This choice is dependent on every man and woman and is interdependent on all of us moving collectively towards our greater good.

"It has been our privilege to get to know the wonderful human beings who have been featured in SoulVision Magazine."

BK Fulton
Founding Chairman, CEO
SOULIDIFLY
PRODUCTIONS

VCU
VIRGINIA COMMONWEALTH UNIVERSITY

VCU da Vinci Center Address

SPEECHES
1992-2020

OCTOBER 10, 1992

WHAT YOUNG BLACK MEN NEED FROM THE MALE AND FEMALE HEADS OF FAMILIES

I would like to begin by thanking Reverend Richardson again for inviting us out today, our President - John Jacob - for setting the tone this morning, Richard Brown for his words of wisdom and that generous introduction, and to all of you for making this important event a part of your busy lives.

Reiterate RB's accomplishments - VP, Deputy Commissioner, Harvard M. ED., Professor at Wesleyan College - and that he was told not to go to college. Outline my accomplishments - HYPE, New School M.Sc. and Sloan Fellow, EBONY 30 Leaders, 1 of 15 world finalists for the Warren Weaver Fellowship at the Rockefeller Foundation - and state that I was told to leave college and join the army. Tell them; "when you see that young boy who looks to be of 'little promise', look again."

WHAT'S AHEAD FOR BLACK MEN: THE CHALLENGE AND THE CURE?...

Ironically, you; this audience; is both the "challenge and the cure." In your minds and veins flows the elements of the antidote for our salvation.

Inherent in the collective excellence in this room, are enough models of success to generate an army of responsible African American males. With your help young African American men will blaze a path of leadership and individual self-discipline paralleled only by the examples of our ancestors and the splendor of your present-day accomplishments. You are the tour guides. You have the road maps The challenge is to bring these road maps out; to share the plan; to lift every young brother up. I know you can do it. Your grandparents did it before you. And each time black men and women have worked together to lift themselves and their families, this nation was lifted; the world was lifted.

HOW DO WE LIFT OURSELVES?...

Well, we must harness and take on attitudes like that of Mary McCloud Bethune - a long time Urban Leaguer. The spirit that convinced her to go to a place; see the need for a college; and with less than $2.00, commit to building a college; and then do it!; is the type of spirit that is without question, a part of the cure.

I know, some of you may be thinking that people are not made out of that "type of stuff" any more. I say to you why not? I contend that the accomplishments of the best of us are characteristic of the potential in all of us. In other words, I encourage you not to focus on the negative. Focusing on the negative does little to yield solutions that ameliorate unfavorable situations facing our communities. For example, focusing on the fact that 1 in 4 black males are under the control of the criminal justice system promotes despair and frustration. Moreover, it does little to contribute to the litany of successes experienced by many black males. In fact, the mass circulation of negative information about our communities masks important observations like . . . if 1 in 4 black males are under the control of the criminal justice system, then 3 in 4 are not!

As we move to empower our communities, part of the challenge is to examine the common denominators that have contributed to the contextual successes of people like yourselves - responsible, courageous, proud black folk.

Don't give me an analysis of a lunatic, instill in me the resilience of the Honorable L. Douglas Wilder, the character of John Jacob, the mentorship of Richard Brown, the tenacity and foresight of David Dinkins, the common sense of Harriet Tubman, the spirit of Mary McCloud Bethune, the fervor of Reverend Richardson, the integrity of Reverend Gray. Give me some of what these people have . . . and watch me fly.

We need an intergenerational movement. Movements are built on the hopes of positive outcomes. No one will rally around tragedy and despair. Indicators of tragedy - frustration and despair - lend to attitudes of apathy, narcissism, and misinterpreting the aspiring victor as a victim.

Indicators of success - optimism, and progress- on the other hand, contribute to feelings of partnership, togetherness, and hope. These things are the cornerstones of a movement.

We need an intergenerational movement. Turn tragedy into triumph. Turn oppression into opportunity. Turn your life into a vehicle that guides our young boys towards leadership and ownership of the 21st Century.

And with God as our witness, if the statisticians tell us that "on every social indicator we are on average at the bottom of life's totem pole", then we should answer, "on average then, we are strategically positioned to grasp our community at the root of its core, and LIFT IT UP . . . LIFT IT UP, LIFT IT UP!

We need you to recreate in us, the brilliance, the wisdom, the genius that is in you. You have the road maps. It is your individual duty to shape the next wave of brothers, husbands, and fathers. It is our collective duty - as black men - to take our wives, families and communities on a journey towards the zenith of human potential. I am proud to be a black man. I'm proud to be African American in the 1990's. I said I am proud to be a black man. One more time for the record - I am proud to be a black man!

It all begins by cultivating in our boys the type of positive attitudes that brought you here today. It is written that "he who can walk with kings and yet maintain the common touch . . . yours is the earth and everything that's in it . . . and -- which is more -- you will be a man, . . . " We must be timely with our efforts too. It is true that conditions are not at an optimum. But have they ever been? We would all agree that when our ancestors arrived here in chains more than 300 years ago, conditions were not optimum. We could all agree that when many of you chose to endure the indignity of going through back doors and drinking at "black only" water fountains, that conditions were not optimum. This conference is just outside of NYC, where the Honorable Mayor David N. Dinkins presides. I am sure that we could agree that in 1990, when he became the first African American Mayor to lead the great city of New York, conditions were not optimum. No . . . not optimum. Will conditions ever be optimum? I contend not . . . yet we move forward. The time to act is now. Start right where you are, shake a hand, make a friend - kiss your child, spread the word . . . "everything is gonna be all right."

DON'T WAIT FOR THE OPTIMUM TIME . . . CREATE IT!

Black men come from a legacy of turning great tragedy into triumph. We take what we have and optimize it.

When one takes just a little time out to train and shape the men who must carry our torch into tomorrow, you are doing your part for the empowerment of our communities. In this frame of mind; this modus operandi; life means more than the flow of currency, life means more than a nice house, a brand new car - in this modus operandi life is an opportunity to live out a purpose, to manifest your legacy, to recreate yourself in others.

What better purpose than to contribute to the world a responsible African American man! You see we all must "check out" at some point. When I check out, I want to leave behind a cadre of responsible, gainfully employed, and well educated warriors who are so "checked-in", that my family is safe, and I in turn can, . . . "rest in peace."

Black men make the world better by making themselves better. In fact, each time black men have stood up, we have pushed this nation to stand up and walk a little straighter. If you don't think it so then consider the life of Nat Turner, consider the life of Frederick Douglass, consider the life of Martin Luther King, consider the life of Malcom X; . . . Consider yourself and what you have done to make things better. Consider your life a commitment to the excellence ..., the legacy ... of proud black men.

Some nay sayers may ask why then, . . . "why if black men are so great are your casualties so high - you're in jail, you drop out, you die of hypertension?" I say to them that it is often risky to be on the front lines, in the vanguard, in the trenches. It is risky to be a pioneer. It is risky to be number one. But we are. Again it is our legacy to shape the world and make it better. You know what I am talking about. I am asking you to increase your efforts at preparing the next generation, my generation, to "receive the baton." When you reached back to receive the baton for your generation - you made a commitment to African manhood. In doing so, you aligned yourself with our great ancestors to receive the existential tools that God has made our birthright.

By reaching forward to pass that baton - what you will be doing is passing our collective legacy forward to those who must take it further. And by doing so, you will have sufficiently completed your "leg" for the race.

In closing, I would like to share with you something I wrote as I watched parts of Los Angeles burn: One of the greatest ways to protest is with massive success. Long term success often involves a more sophisticated form of conflict, education, debate, and calculated confrontation — but still these things capture the essence of substantive protest. It is easy to become engulfed in the negative when things look bad. Too often we allow our journey through the bowels of this world to overshadow the beacons of light that keep us going. Too often we fail to see incidents of horror as windows of opportunity. The poem you are about to hear is a testament to the fact that there are many good men who are still true to our movement. True enough, these men are rising alongside powerful women in spite of the obstacles placed before them.

Let us focus on and reproduce the energies, the supports that help these souls to rise.
It is time.

FORCE VITALE

If not now! . . . when?

Do you feel the spirit rising in us?

. . . around us.

The Brothers are back!

New men.

Spiritual men.

Men who define themselves.

Men who do not buckle in the face of adversity.

Men who love their women.

Men who love their children.

Men who love their world.

Men who love themselves.

Like great rocks that rise out of solid ground

. . . we move forward - unafraid.

I thank God almighty that I am alive

. . . to be a part of this movement.

It is no longer enough that we survive.

It is time to develop and prosper.

On the strength of your and my ancestors

. . . before we are through

. . . this world will be a better place.

Brian. K

NOTE:
This speech was delivered to an audience of men and women at Grace Baptist Church in Mount Vernon, NY (10/10/92). The speech was prepared for the Church's regional conference, "What's Ahead For Black Men: The Challenge And The Cure." The morning session theme, "Black Male Empowerment Through Family Structure", was the sub-theme for this address. Other expected presenters for the conference include the Honorable L. Douglas Wilder, Earl G. Graves, the Honorable David N. Dinkins, John E. Jacob, Reverend Benjamin L. Hooks, and the Reverend Jesse Jackson. Reverend W. Franklyn Richardson, D.D. (an NUL Board member) made the request for an African American Adolescent Male Development Center presentation at the conference. Richard Brown (62 years old) and Karee Brown (12 years old) also presented at this session. The session was video taped.

JUNE 18, 1997

STEP-BY-STEP: ON GRADUATION DAY

I appreciate that very generous introduction. I hope I can live up to that . . . . I am really honored to be here. I would like to begin by thanking Principal James Duffy, Martin Kenny, Ernie Pitts and the teachers and staff for inviting me out today. Principal Duffy and I have become e-mail buddies. He really believes in you and he loves this school. You are blessed to have him here. Each of you should also be sure to thank your parents and loved ones for all the support over the years; and we should all thank our Creator for blessing us to be here this morning.

I have 3 goals today. First, I hope to have a little fun talking about my journey . . . step-by-step to graduation; second I hope to be brief, I am told that I have just a few minutes to say what I have to say, and further I have been told that long graduation addresses put everybody to sleep; finally, I hope to share something useful that you can take with you for the rest of your lives.

When I graduated from Dozier Middle school in 1980, I thought that was the hardest thing I had ever done.

Then I went to Denbigh High School. I decided, just for a minute, that that was the hardest . . . until I went to Va Tech for College. Graduating from college took a lot of work and five long years. I figured that made it the toughest thing I had ever done.

Graduate school -- you know, what people who don't have jobs do after they go to college – is what brought me to New York City. That took 2 years, but since I was away from home, I decided that that was the hardest thing.

Then I started law school at night in 1994. Everybody told me that that was the hardest thing. But you know what, I told myself, to take it step-by-step. That's how life works. When you put one foot in front of the other one, you usually make it to wherever you want to go. Today, you are taking a big step towards being whatever you want to be.

We know you are going to be great. The man this school is named after, Dr. Daniel Hale Williams, was a great man. Did you know that in 1891 he founded the first interracial hospital in the United States? Did you know that in 1893 he performed the world's first known open heart surgery? Well he did.

He was creative, artistic, and talented . . . just like all of you are. I am sure that some folk told him it was going to be hard, or that he could not do it, but he did . . . step-by-step.

My experiences and Dr. William's story have taught me that life is not always "easy." It takes perseverance, hard work and determination to reach any worthy goal. Most importantly, all of us are here because someone helped us along the way. Life is about helping others to help themselves.

So to the teachers and counselors, you must continue to believe in your students. You must have high expectations of them and support their dreams as if they were your own. Our society has changed. When most of the adults in this room went to school, the world economy was dominated by big industry and manufacturing. Now knowledge, services and information dominate the world. This means that great teachers will have to embrace the right balance of books and technology as they prepare students for 21st Century. This means that you will have to embrace new skills and new tools. This means that you will have to be a coach in the classroom. This means that most classrooms will have to become laboratories that promote and encourage the exchange of ideas with other classrooms in your school, as well as with schools across the globe.

To the parents and loved ones, I ask that you continue to support your children with positive words of encouragement and some of your time. Being a teenager "ain't what it used to be." Today, many distractions like the lure of being "cool," drugs, gangs, and the pressure to just fit-in, compete for your children's attention. These things take our young people, our future, down a highway of disappointment.

On the other hand, with your continued support of your child's dreams and the school's programs, the young people here will soar like eagles on the world's "Information Superhighway." Just to be clear, in practical terms, this means that you may have to buy that home computer; or stop in to help the school to wire classrooms. This could also mean that you spend a few nights a week helping with homework or e-mailing the principal. In short, we all must commit to being active contributors to the achievement of our young leaders. Today's graduation is an important step into "tomorrow."

Finally, to the students . . . I ask that you keep giving education your best. Remember . . . , you are not going to school for your mother or your father, family or your friends. You are going to school for yourself. I remember when I was failing out of college, it did not feel so good. Then someone told me to try going to class and reading the books!

All of a sudden I started doing well. I started to believe in myself. Learning became fun. I knew then that I was setting the stage for my own future. I went from the probation list to the Dean's list. As a result, today I travel all over the country helping people to use computers and the Internet to change their lives.

"All I had to do was to decide to do my best."

Now it's "all good." Eleven years ago, I had a dream to become a lawyer, and exactly eleven days ago (June 8th, 1998), I graduated from law school! Show me some love please (clap or do a "raise the roof" sign).

In closing, it has been an honor to address you on this important day. You have all done well and now it is time to celebrate that achievement. Middle School 180, Class of 1998 . . . Young Leaders of the 21st Century . . . I charge you to go forth and to do your very best. Congratulations on a job well done!

Thank you.

This speech was delivered to an audience of approximately 250 students, their families, educators and staff at the 1998 Graduation Ceremony of the School for Fine Arts (M.S. 180 6/18/98). Ernie Pitts (VP for Simon and Schuster's SBG Publishing subsidiary) and James Duffy (Principal) arranged for my participation.

JUNE 13, 2006

DREAM

Most speakers refer to this in their graduation talks. You'll hear comments such as Dare to be different.

Dream it and Do it.

Today, I will try to give you what I hope will be something easy to remember if you want to. I've made the word **DREAM** into an acronym, so that each letter stands for something significant.

D – DO SOMETHING YOU LIKE/LOVE.

In your job, in your community service, in your hobbies. You will be happier as will those around you. But the catch is you have to DO something. Life is not for couch potatoes. It's hard to be effective if you're always a spectator. Let me give you an example in Charleston. It was something formed in 1982, while providing medical care at St. John's Episcopal Church Manna Meal program. Now patient visits have grown to 67,000; 100,000 RX's have been filled for seniors, the working poor, the homeless; it has 27 specialty clinics; and every dollar donated results in $30 dollars of in-kind support and health services. Who or what is this? WV Health Right.

I happened to know this is a labor of love for Pat White, a former legislator. She is passionate about her cause and this organization is worthwhile and doing a great job of meeting some of the medical needs of the needy. They have countless volunteers, a diverse group of practitioners and many benefactors. Back then, back when, some 24 years ago, some folks decided they had to do something.

Billy Crystal, in the movie "City Slickers" learned from Jack Palance, the cowboy and cattle herder, that each of us has to find out the one thing to be happy in life. When Billy asked Palance what is the one thing, Palance answered, that's what you have to figure out. Whatever you do is up to you. I can only encourage you to like and love it. I work in public affairs for Verizon and love what I do. I also love working with the WVCNCS and promoting Volunteer WV.

R – RECOGNIZE OTHERS AND THEIR ACCOMPLISHMENTS.

Say thank you. Work through others and your peers. Because you can't do it, whatever it is, alone. I haven't met anybody of any stature or station in life who does not want to be thanked for his or her contributions, commitment to a cause, or part in making something happen. Home Depot likes to advertise "you can do it and we can help." If you internalize this slogan, it might be, you can do it and other people can and will help you." So be sure and recognize them.

Personal example – my hospital stay in 2004. Two months. Almost died. Angels helped me. Visits, prayers, etc. They took the time to care. I wrote many personal t/y notes. Had more visitors than anybody said one nurse.

E – EXPECT MORE OF YOURSELF AND OTHERS.

Set some stretch objectives when you do it or something. Example – O.J. Simpson running back. Ran for 2,000 yards. His offensive guard, Reggie McKenzie, first had the dream and told OJ we'll block for you and we'll achieve it, and they did.

You've heard it said that some people step up to the challenge, when faced with adversity or stress or a problem. I believe this. Have you ever wondered how to handle a big problem or make a big decision? I would submit to you it might start with some faith and the notion of expecting more.

If you've heard of the Parretto principle, it says 80% of everything is done by 20% of the people. They say this applies to work, volunteering, philanthropy and so on. I consider myself to be in the 20% category and suggest you should be there. And don't settle for excluding the rest of the people. Many times you just have to ask for help and some people won't do it or something until you do ask.

A – ACKNOWLEDGE YOUR MISTAKES AND ASSESS YOUR STRENGTHS.

In my own case, I would never make an engineer or work on the technical side of our business. I made a personal discovery about 10 years ago. We are what we are and we aint what we aint. My God-given talents revolve around speaking and writing and communicating and creating. I've always worked in PR and public affairs. I lobby for a living.

On a personal note, I play rhythm guitar and sing back-up in our church contemporary musical group. Notice I didn't say, play lead or sing lead. I'm mostly back-up and content to play that role. However, together, using everyone's talents and strengths, we make some good music. Assessing and using your strengths is one thing, but the acknowledging our mistakes comes hard for most people. Edison did not let it bother him that some of his inventions failed before he invented the light bulb. He kept going and ultimately prevailed. You've heard it said, if you haven't ever failed at something, you probably haven't tried. I've made mistakes on the job, in personal relationships, in making music.

What's important is to learn from them and move forward.

M – MAKE A DIFFERENCE.

This is a companion corollary to the first one, do something. Have the attitude that if it is to be, it's up to me. I used to have this saying in church that God never called anybody to do everything, but He did call everybody to something. I was referring to getting folks to volunteer for a project. In the same way, the governor is big on community service and I've heard him say, what have You done for your community lately?

President Bush said "the public good depends on private character ... That character is formed and shaped by institutions like family, faith, and the many civil, social and civic organizations, from the Boy Scouts to the local Rotary club." Comedian George Carlin commented we've been to the moon and back, but we have trouble crossing the street to meet a new neighbor. Sometimes making a difference is doing something small for a neighbor in need.

Actor Tom Hanks spoke last year at Vassar's commencement. He related his "power of four" theme. When asked how many cars would have to be taken off the road to turn a completely jammed freeway into a free-flowing one, researchers did a computer simulation and determined the answer was four cars out of 100. Hanks called that the power of 4. He went on to say if 4 out of 100 people could remove gridlock by not using their cars, imagine the other changes that can be wrought by just 4 of us, 4 of you out of a hundred. Hanks said the power of 4 is the difference between helplessness and help.

If I took a survey here today, I'd probably learn most of you already know the elements of the big DREAM – Doing something you like; recognizing the importance of others and teams to your success; expecting more of yourself even when you don't think you have it to give; acknowledging and learning from your mistakes and assessing and utilizing your strengths, and finally making a difference.

That's partly why we're here. To celebrate your achievements to date, your graduation from Appalread, and maybe to encourage you to dream about your future a bit.

Before I close, I must acknowledge I was and am impressed by your collective accomplishments at Appalread. Americorps members breaking the cycle of illiteracy. Affecting the academic performance of 3,000 young people. One on one tutoring in reading and writing (something near and dear to my heart). All of the training you went through. All of the volunteers you recruited. Appalread is well recognized as a success and a collaborative effort because of you and others in the education field, the business community, the non-profits, and the faith-based community.

You should be proud of your achievements. I would only ask you to remember to give something back, to remember the **DREAM** if you can. I'm reminded of one more person who said something I will never forget. Actor Kevin Spacey was asked who helped him become a successful actor. He replied Jack Lemmon, now deceased, was his mentor. And the advice Lemmon gave Spacey? When you've made it the top of your field, remember to send the elevator back down for somebody else. In other words, give back, pay it forward.

You've had help along the way of life, so don't forget to help others.

I congratulate each of you and hope you have sweet dreams tonight and for the rest of your life. Thanks for having me here today.

This speech was delivered by my friend and colleague Sam Cipoletti in Logan, WV at Southern Community College. The audience numbered 50-100 and included G.E.D. program graduates and their families. The speech is reprinted here with Sam's permission. I hope it inspires you the same way it inspired me.

DECEMBER 21, 2008

EXPANDING THE CIRCLES OF LIFE

I appreciate that very generous introduction. I hope I can live up to that . . . . I am really honored to be here. I would like to begin by thanking the organizers for inviting me to this special occasion – especially Dr. Hazo Carter – a man I am honored to call a friend. Of course, I extend my congratulations to all the graduates of West Virginia State University and West Virginia State Community & Technical College. It is an honor to be here with you and your families this afternoon. Today is a great day indeed.

This is my first commencement address since we have been in West Virginia. I get chills when I think of the history of West Virginia State. Dr. Hazo and First Lady Phyllis Carter, I know you are proud of what you have achieved. Part of the role of a commencement speaker is to keep people awake through what can be a long ceremony; so I will try to do that. Another thing that a good speaker should do is to say something that matters. So I will try to do that as well. Since I am a business man, allow me to get one commercial out of the way – (tap mic) "can you here me now?" That was for my friends at Verizon. Now, let's get down to graduation business.

In light of why we have gathered here today, to honor those who have earned the right and privilege of commencement, I felt inspired to talk about what each of us must do to help West Virginia to be all that it can be. My theme for today is "Expanding the Circles of Life."

It's a simple question to ask, but it can take a lifetime to determine – how big is your circle? I recently reflected on the idea of a circle of life while watching a movie. It was an average movie, but the story of the circle was extraordinary. It went something like this:

A young man from a prehistoric tribe asked the tribal leader, what kind of man was my father? The tribal leader knew that the young man was curious as to why his father left the village when he was just a little boy. The tribal leader responded –

"A good man draws a circle around himself and his family. He cares for them, provides for them, and will risk his life for them. A great man, draws a circle around his community. The circle includes his family, his brother, and his neighbors. He cares for them, provides for them, and will at times, risk his life for them. The greatest of men draw an even larger circle around the multitudes. The circle includes his family, his brother, his neighbors and strangers. He cares for them, provides for them, and will at times risk his life for them. This is the kind of man that your father was. **It is up to you to decide what kind of man you will be.**"

One of the things I like most about this concept is that it starts with a "good man." There is no lower option. It is assumed that you will at least take care of your responsibilities, so aim high. In these tough economic times, our great state will need your sharp minds and talents more than ever.The other thing that I really like about the circle of life concept is that it reminds us that we have the power to choose how broad our reach will be. Some of us leave important decisions about our future to others instead of exercising our right to choose who and what we will become. Tough times call for the best in all of us to stand up. We stand tall when we stand for ourselves and others. We stand tallest when we stand for what is right. And let me be clear, if you don't decide to stand for something, you will fall for anything.

Today, I am the President of Verizon West Virginia. However, I was not always on the leadership track. There was a time when some folk probably thought I was on anything but the right track? I was not standing for the right things. My decision to apply to college back in 1984 was not for the best of reasons. Quite simply, my friends were going to VA Tech; in coming engineers at Tech could force their parents to purchase a computer as part of their required school supply; and I had heard that VA Tech was a "good-school" (all in that order).

One might have guessed that I was not as serious or as focused as I should have been (and one would have guessed right). My daily activity in my first years at college consisted of 12-13 hours of required sleep, huge doses of computer video games, as much basketball as my body could stand, and as many girlfriends as would have me . . . oh, and food, and classes (in that order). The average of my first year's grades was terribly below "C" level. I was flunking out fast. The next summer, and I think the one after that, I took as much pottery, advanced pottery, and extremely advanced pottery as the school offered. A little planning would have told me that 2 summers of "B" grades would not serve as a sufficient counter balance for two years of near "D" grades. By the end of my second year at Tech my grade point average was still shabby, and I was bitter. I became a charter member of the "gripe club." I was consumed by the notion that Tech was not good for me. I had decided to quit college and was considering joining the Army. One big problem was that I did not know how to leave. What would my parents say? ... my friends ... my professors. I decided that it would be best for me to "cruise" through one more semester of "easy classes" while I planned my escape from VA Tech.

Notwithstanding the frequent academic warning notes I received from the Registrar's Office, it was the "D" I received in a Human Sexual Development course that gave me a life-altering wake-up call. How could I get a "D" in Human Sexual Development? At that point, my time at Tech became personal. I asked myself "who am I?"; "where did I want to go?"; and "who could help me to get there?" One loud and clear answer was that I wanted to graduate!

I immediately drafted a "declaration of independence" from my parents. Accept for continued and much appreciated tuition payments, I reported to my folks that I was now on my own. I had resolved to go to class and to do "my best" ... not for grades ... but to do my best. It's amazing what happens when you actually read the assignments and show up to class prepared.

To expand your circles, you have to show up.

I also adjusted my priorities; changed majors (I really did not like engineering, I just wanted the computer); I read extra books; visited my professors; took courses that peaked my curiosity; met with other "serious" students; assigned myself extra homework, and narrowed my dating habits down to one lady. I was on a mission. Guess what, My GPA sky-rocketed! Tremendous self-confidence came with my swelling GPA.

Excellence became my standard mode of operation. Again, school had become a personal matter. I took Honors courses; made the Dean's List, joined student organizations and took office; I even took that Human Sexual Development course over and got a B+! I also found value in volunteering and mentoring other students in excellence!

I was a new man. These developments in my attitude and thinking are the cornerstones for all that I have achieved to-date. In fact, before I left Tech, I had academic scholarships to the top 25 management and policy analysis schools in the country. You may be asking yourself "how did he make such a dramatic change?"

The answer is simple. By shifting my focus away from all the negatives and by reaching out to my professors and many others who were willing to help me to help myself, I was able to change my attitude towards the university and my personal expectations about graduation. While I did not graduate Cum Laude, I did graduate "thank you Lordy!" Later, I also went on to graduate with high honors from graduate school and law school.

Our minds are like funnels.

When I was doubting myself and thinking about quitting, I was taking in information at the little end of the funnel. When I decided that I would do my very best in school, I began to take in information from the big end of the funnel.

A new world opened up to me. The library became one of my favorite places. In our current Information Age economy, we all have an opportunity to reach out to the world. Technologies like High Speed Internet and the World Wide Web challenge us to be our best and to seek out the best in others.

I remember the first time I was on CNN talking about a "digital campus" project that I was working on with Verizon (the company was called NYNEX at the time). My Mom called me excited saying "baby, you were on TV all day today; I'm so proud of you!" Well now I run Verizon West Virginia.

So what does all this have to do with serving West Virginia? I'm getting to it. When my family and I first came to WV just over a year ago, we did not know what to expect. We spent time with leaders like Gov. Manchin, Dr. Carter, and many others to get a sense of what West Virginia was about. We also talked to teachers, ministers, other parents and folk we met as we settled in. One thing was common, the people here are exceptional. The landscapes are spectacular. It's easy to love West Virginia. I have to share a story that really brings this point home.

One snowy night last winter my twins and I were driving home from a talk I gave at St. Albans Elementary. The 5th grade class there had won an international award for 21st Century learning and Dr. Steve Paine wanted a member of industry there to share some thoughts with the youngsters, their parents and other caring adults.

The snow had built up pretty heavily during the course of the event. By the time my boys and I got back to Teays Valley, the roads had become very slippery and dangerous. The turn up a hill towards our home had become treacherous due to ice and snow. However, being the man that I am, I figured that we could simply rev the HEMI engine and make it up the ice covered approach. It did not work. And my car slid backwards for a few yards, just narrowly missing a large ditch. We were stuck. I called out to God, and said "Lord, we were just doing your work right there in St. Albans, please don't leave me out here to sit on a school night with my boys. My wife will kill me." I waited for a response.

A few minutes later, a car pulled up behind me and three men got out. They all had beards and caps on. One had on flip flops. If I were in another state I would have prepared to fight, but I stayed calm as one of them approached my car and tapped on the window. He said, "We will push you up the hill." And that's exactly what they did. They were good West Virginians. Those young men embody the spirit of the state. They drew a broad circle that night.

As I said, it's easy to love West Virginia. The harder thing to do is to serve West Virginia. This is where more of us need to draw our circles large. Why do I say we need to focus on service to our great state? Here is what the most current data tells us:

IN HEALTH:

- WV has the 10th highest infant mortality rate in the nation.

- 3rd highest proportion of overweight and obese adults in the nation.

- Our proportion of adults with diabetes and hypertension exceeds the national average.

IN WORKFORCE DEVELOPMENT:

- WV suffers from low K-12 student performance in reading, writing and math.

- Our state has a lower adult education attainment, compared to the national workforce.

IN R&D AND ENTREPRENEURSHIP:

- WV ranks 50th in inventor patents;

- 46th in industry patents; and

- 49th in entrepreneurial activity.

CLEARLY, WE HAVE SOME WORK TO DO. HOWEVER, I AM AN OPTIMIST BY NATURE AND THERE ARE MANY GOOD THINGS TO BUILD ON:

- WV currently leads the nation in economic development.

- WV has a low cost of living and the highest homeownership rate in nation (75%).

- WV has great people and a natural beauty that causes it to be known as the "Switzerland of the South."

- WV's investment in technology, professional development for teachers, and other administrative policies puts the state among the best in the nation;

- WV had the highest increase of advanced placement scores in the nation; . . . And

Today you have graduated.

These good things about WV are things we can build on. They are worthy of our largest circles.

> To make our circles large, we have to work together. Each of us has something to bring to the table right now that can make WV better. In case you are wondering what you can do, let me share some thoughts.

EDUCATORS:

- You must expect the most of all of the students in your circle and help them to acquire a thirst for lifelong learning. You must help them to be so good, that they can replace you when it's time. Our young people will rise to the challenge. I have found it to be true that a mind once expanded by great ideas never returns to its original dimensions.

PARENTS:

- Remember to give your sons and daughters room to reach the stars. You have raised some of the most talented young leaders in the state. Now, you have to trust in the values that you have instilled and give them the respect that they have earned. If you hold them too close, you risk constraining the very wings that can take them towards the zenith of their potential.

GOVERNMENT LEADERS:

- Draw your circles wide. Remember, you uphold the public interest. In our democratic society, the people count on Government to make sure that all of us have an equal opportunity to live, work and prosper.

BUSINESS LEADERS:

- Invest in West Virginia. Work works. Encourage your employees to give back to their communities. Do well and do good by winning the right way.

These ideas for serving West Virginia are within our reach. I have great faith that we all can do something. We all can do more. I believe that to whom much is given, much is expected (Luke 12:48). When I was younger, I thought the "much" was a specific thing – an ability to sing, dance, jump high, or play an instrument for example. As I matured I realized that the "much" was actually life itself. If you woke up this morning (that would be all of us here today) . . . ,

If you woke up this morning, you have been given a great gift.

YOU HAVE LIFE.

Whether you are old or young, male or female, fully able or have some disabilities, if you woke up, you are on the hook. No excuses.

Your job is to live your life to its fullest potential; to draw your circles wide.

You see, if a person with a funny name can become President . . . (pause) of Verizon, so can you.

I was blessed to learn this lesson about life and the power of working together when I was a young man. My confidence in our capacity to draw large circles emanates from my little sister who can not walk or talk.

I will close with a poem I wrote in her honor.

SHAUNA

A gazing little boy stopped and asked

Can you run?

Yes, adjusting her leg brace.

Can you dance?

Yes, adjusting her position in her wheelchair.

Are you happy?

Yes, adjusting her gaze towards heaven.

Big brother, now that you are a man, in your new-found wisdom, don't count me out.

I run in my mind, I am an Olympian.

I dance in my dreams, I am a Debutante.

And I am happy . . . , because I am alive.

Thank you. Congratulations on your achievement. Please draw big circles around each other, West Virginia and our Nation.

God bless you all.

NOTE:

This commencement address was delivered to an audience of approximately 4,000 guests at West Virginia State University's, 2008 December Commencement.

FEBRUARY 2, 2013

DOING THE WORK

Ken, thank you for that kind introduction. Oliver, thank you and the MBL board for selecting me to give this year's keynote address. My friend Ken Ampy, CEO of Astyra Corporation and MBL Board Chair, did a marvelous job last year as the keynote. I hope I can be half as good as he was. I have a number of friends in the audience so I will not try to identify everyone. I'll just welcome you all and thank you for coming out this evening for a night of inspiration, recognition and celebration. I would like to acknowledge my parents and other special guests sitting at my table. Welcome.

Oliver, is it OK if I take off my jacket? . . . . No, I'm not going to get naked up here. My point, other than getting comfortable with my extended family, is to demonstrate our common elements. You see, in life, once we take off the garments of our stations, we are mostly the same. Man or woman, black or white, rich or poor; when it comes to our entrepreneurial potential, we are relative equals. What sets us apart are our core beliefs and whether or not we have the courage to act on those beliefs. In other words, are we willing to Do the Work? In fact, my theme for this evening is – Doing the Work.

On the 21st of January, when our nation celebrates the birthday of Martin Luther King, Jr., I had the pleasure of attending the inauguration of our 44th President, Barack Obama. It was a humbling experience. I was there with friends and loved ones. I was struck by the awesome specter of it all, 100s of thousands in the crowd, millions watching on TV, and billions around the globe tuning in on radios, and other devices to witness the second installation of an African American as President of these United States. I think it's fitting to start off with a prayer if you don't mind?

Dear Lord, thank you for allowing us to be the dreams of our ancestors. Thank you for allowing us to be role models for the generations to follow. And Lord, thank you for opening the eyes of everyone here today; we know it's a blessing to be on the right side of the dirt. May we always remember that the gifts we enjoy each day are because of your goodness and mercy. Finally Lord, I pray that my words this evening provide some value for those gathered here and please use us as the instruments of a brighter tomorrow. And one more thing Lord, thank you that this meeting is not on Super Bowl Sunday! In your Son's name we pray. Amen.

VERIZON STORY

As I stated earlier, my theme this evening is "Doing the Work." I'd like to tell you about a company that is well known today, but it was not so well known 20 years ago. In fact, it did not even exist. The company I'm talking about is my own.

THE VERIZON TRANSFORMATION: A 20-YEAR JOURNEY

Verizon was created in 2000, but the companies that formed its core business go back more than a century. If you looked at Bell Atlantic and NYNEX 20 years ago you would see very different companies, in what was a very different communications industry:

- Revenues were one-quarter of their current size;

- We were a local landline company based in 14 states in the northeast and mid-Atlantic;

- The Wireless revolution was just starting – with a couple of million customers in our region;

- We had NO global business;

- Legacy technologies in both landline and wireless limited the range of products we could offer;

- Despite the emergence of the Worldwide Web in 1993-94, VZ's 1997 annual report didn't even mention the word "Internet";

- We were highly regulated at the federal and state levels, making it easy for non-regulated competitors to freely pick off profitable services, and leave legacy services to us.

We found ourselves in a changing world where consumer expectations had shifted from . . . . Analog to digital.   Photos, movies, books, newspapers, money, health records ... all of it was converting to "x's" and "o's" and flowing over the Internet.

Customers started demanding access to everything from everywhere, especially their hand-held devices. Essentially, the tangible world was turning into a giant information system or what we call in the industry a "digital ecosystem" and people started carrying their digital lives with them wherever they went [HOLD UP PHONE].

A CHANGING WORLD: NEW INVESTOR EXPECTATIONS

Like customers, investor expectations also changed. The old predictable utility world gave way to a more dynamic competitive environment:

So we've gone from . . . .

- A Utility industry to technology industry;

- A Monopoly mindset to competitive mindset;

- Rate-of-return regulation to market-driven growth; and

- Low risk/ low returns, to higher risk, and higher returns.

GROWTH OF BROADBAND , 07-12

What's more, the technologies and businesses driving Verizon's growth today barely existed 15 years ago. The World's Internet population has doubled in the last 5 years, to 2.3 B – that's more than a billion new users in 5 years

As fast as the number of users is growing, Internet traffic is growing even faster.

- Global IP traffic is up eightfold over the past 5 years and will triple over the next 5 years.

- In 2016, the gigabyte equivalent of all movies ever made will cross global IP networks every 3 minutes.

And the biggest driver of this explosion of innovation is the demand for mobility:

- There are more than 6 Billion mobile subscribers in the world (2011)

- Wireless penetration exceeds 100 percent in the U.S. – yes, there are more devices than there are people.

TWO CHOICES: BUILD OR SELL?

So there we were:

- Geographically constricted in a globalizing industry;

- A regulated utility with limited cash for investment in growth markets;

- An analog company in a digitizing era; and

- A declining core business with an unsustainable cost structure.

In short, we were in trouble. We had to decide what to do with these still-valuable but rapidly depreciating assets: Build or sell?

To start, we determined that we wanted to control our own destiny and remake our company for the future. To be one of the survivors in a restructuring communications industry we determined that we needed to roll up our sleeves and do four big things:

- First, gain scale and scope through a series of mergers and acquisitions;

- Second, make our networks a platform for growth by investing in broadband, mobile and global IP;

- Third, make our core business viable again by reinventing our product set and reforming our cost structure; and

- Fourth, transforming our relationship with customers through marketing, and enhancing our brand and corporate culture.

CHALLENGE – GLOBALIZE AND GAIN SCALE

- To realize our vision we decided to grow our national footprint through the Bell Atlantic, NYNEX and GTE mergers, plus several wireless acquisitions.

- We achieved global reach and access to a multinational customer base through the acquisition of MCI.

- We added vertical capabilities and solutions expertise through smaller deals such as acquiring Cybertrust, Terremark, CloudSwitch, and Hughes Communications.

- We integrated many companies under a single brand and corporate structure.

CHALLENGE – INVEST FOR GROWTH

We essentially leapfrogged the market by investing nearly $20B to deploy superior networks like 4G, FiOS and advanced Cloud services.

It took a lot of work to get here and we continue to engage on all aspects of our plans. So what result did we achieve? Not only has the revenue pie grown, but the growth profile of the company has been transformed. Our center of gravity has shifted dramatically to growth markets and our market valuations are at all-time highs:

- In 2006: More than half our revenues were from the traditional legacy telephone business;

- By 2011: Almost two-thirds of our revenues came from wireless; with legacy business revenues down to 22 percent;

TODAY WE ARE . . . .

- #15 on the Fortune 500.

- The largest U.S. wireless company, with over 100 M retail customers.

- We have 5.3 M FiOS Internet customers and 4.6 M FiOS Video customers.

- And we provide communications, entertainment and advanced business solutions to 99% of Fortune 1000.

You can see why I am proud to lead the Virginia companies for Verizon. When we started doing business in Virginia almost 100 years ago, we were just another small business trying to make it. We literally strung wires over the tops of buildings downtown. We may have had 50 customers. How things change. Today, small businesses are second only to the church in changing lives. There are approximately 27 million small business owners in the U.S. Collectively, these businesses create between 60% - 70% of net new jobs in the US each year.

What's the difference between the small businesses that do succeed and those that do not? . . . . Doing the Work.

I've been in business in one form or another since I was a child. I started cutting grass with my Dad when I was about 10 years old. While child labor remains illegal, I don't fault my father for teaching me how to put a few coins in my pocket. Landscaping was honest work and it kept me off the streets and helped me to get in shape for football and basketball. Years later, I even learned how to borrow my Dad's customers, tools and equipment so that I could branch off on my own. Thanks Dad.

My parents got me ready for business and the world by teaching me to be an optimist. One of my favorite books coming up was *The Little Engine That Could*. You know the story, it's the one about the little steam engine that took on a big job. In short, there was a cargo of toys in "Dreamland" that needed to be hauled over a steep mountain so that the children on the other side could play. The load of toys was heavy and none of the more established or well-known engines offered to help. The little engine took on the task. It repeated, I think I can, I think I can, I think I can, I think I can, I think I can, . . . I can. And it made it over the mountain. While the story was something that taught us the importance of optimism as children, it's worth revisiting as we reflect on "Doing the Work" to make our businesses successful.

Note that the train started out in "Dreamland" – an easy comfortable place. Sometimes it's hard to move from the easy places in life, but if you're going to do something, you have to get up. You have to move forward. You often have to get out of that comfortable place. There is no change without change.

Second, many trains passed on taking the large load up the mountain. They said it was too risky. Well, let me tell you that where there is great risk, there is often great reward. In life, there is always a higher gear. Those that aim high, usually land better than those who do not.

Dr. Benjamin Mays told his students at Morehouse, - "It must be borne in mind that the tragedy of life doesn't lie in not reaching your goal. The tragedy lies in having no goal to reach. It isn't a calamity to die with dreams unfulfilled, but it is a calamity not to dream. It is not a disaster to be unable to capture your ideal, but it is a disaster to have no ideal to capture.

It is not a disgrace not to reach the stars, but it is a disgrace to have no stars to reach for.

Not failure, but low aim is sin."

Last, the objective was to deliver precious cargo to another town for children. Is there anyone here who is not willing to take on something crazy for their children? My Mom is here tonight. Mom, are you crazy for me? Thanks Mom, I love you; you too Dad. The point here is that those of us who really have courage show up. We do the work and we often do it for those to follow; our progeny; our children. As my Grandmother would sometimes say to me, "we did not come here to stay." My friends, I pray that you build your businesses strong so that you leave a lasting legacy.

I know you can do it. If the example of the little engine does not provide enough vicarious stimulation, can-do spirit or motivation, consider the example of Rosa Parks - a seamstress who worked for a small business in Alabama in 1955. On one December day she decided that she was no longer going to sit in the back of the bus. By taking her rightful place, she sparked a movement that changed the world. Don't tell me that we are not capable of moving mountains. It has already been done.

In closing I ask: When you have your opportunity, will you do the work? Will you build your business? Will you deliver for our children? I think you will and I know you can. Thank you again for coming out tonight, thank you for supporting the MBL, and thank you for doing the work!

God bless you all.

NOTE:

These remarks were delivered to an audience of approximately 350 guests at the Metropolitan Business League's 2013 Awards Program. The MBL is the leading organization of minority and women owned businesses in VA (Richmond, VA – 2/2/2013)

REMEMBER THOSE ON THE MARGINS

Thank you for that kind introduction. It is a honor and a privilege to be here today. I feel I am in great company with the next generation of innovators from our community; I believe you will change the world. I have been thinking about what I might say to you that could be of some value. You all are so smart and I'm just a film and technology guy. I know that whatever I say, I better not take too long. Your family is in quarantine and they long to hold you close before you go off to change the world. And you probably have some Zoom partying or Tic-Tocking to do. Is that right? You have a life to live. All of that is good. I'm going to need your help to get through this. Yes, one more "class participation" session and you're really done. My focus this morning is on the people on the margins — the 95% of the world who don't yet know how great they are. If you take anything from my address today, please take this . . . always remember those on the margins.

You may be asking, why would I implore you to remember those on the margins — the poor, people with disabilities, women, minorities, the undereducated and people outside of the economic mainstream? Let me demonstrate with your assistance . . . .

By a show of hands, did anyone turn on a light in your home last night or this morning? Did anyone pass a "red/yellow/ or green" signal light on your way to get food or to check in on a loved one? I do hope you stopped at the red light.

How many of you sent a letter in the mail this week? Does anyone here have a home security system? Keep your hands up. Did anyone recently go to the grocery store for fresh produce (Instacart people, that means you too)? Did anyone turn on a heater during the winter months? Did anyone use a cell phone in the past 24 hours? Do you think medical breakthroughs like blood plasma or open heart surgery are important to humanity? OK, that's it. Thank you for your participation. You all get an A+! I think you know where I am going with this? ALL of the things I just mentioned were created by people on the margins. Let me illuminate just a few of them:

- **The mailbox or "street letter box" as it was called in 1891 was invented by Phillip B. Downing.** Before his invention, people with mail had to go to the post office to drop off letters and packages. Once the mailbox was invented, drop offs could happen at the local street letter box.

- **Refrigerated trucks** were invented by Frederick McKinley Jones in the 1940s. His invention allowed produce in grocery stores to stay fresh.

- The **signal traffic light** was invented by Garrett Morgan in 1923 after he saw a terrible carriage accident. He later sold the patent rights to General Electric for $40,000.

- Marie Van Brittan Brown invented the **home security system** in 1969 in response to high incidents of crime in her Queens neighborhood. Her original design included a video camera. Sound familiar? Can you say Ring doorbell?

- Alice H. Parker invented the **natural heating furnace** in 1919. Today's forced air heating systems are modeled after Ms. Parker's design.

- In the 1970s, Shirley Ann Jackson, the first black woman to receive a PhD from M.I.T., led the team that developed the **touch-tone phone, caller ID and call waiting.** Can you hear me now?

- Dr. Gladys West invented the **GPS,** also known as the **Global Positioning System** and was inducted into the Space and Missile Pioneers Hall of Fame in 2018 by the United States Air Force.

- Mary Sherman Morgan (a.k.a., the Rocket Girl) was a petite woman from North Dakota. She helped to create **rocket fuel**. Her fuel mixture allowed America to win the "Space Race."

- We cannot talk about space without a thankful nod to Ms. Katherine Johnson who passed earlier this year at age 101. Some of her colleagues at NASA thought she was the maid; when in fact, she was a brilliant mathematician – called a "human computer" – who calculated complex **orbital trajectories** by hand. She was memorialized in the Hollywood film "Hidden Figures." Astronaut John Glenn trusted her calculations more than he did the mechanical computers.

- Let's not forget "Amazing Grace" – a.k.a., Ms. Grace Hopper who invented the **first compiler** that allowed computers to talk to each other. She also co-invented **COBOL** – the first commercial programming language widely used in government and business. She was told that ". . . computers only did math." That was true . . . , until it wasn't. Grace developed the system that turned common English words into machine code. Thanks to pioneers like Grace, we are now racing down the roads of artificial intelligence, augmented reality and quantum level computing. Our computers can now order groceries, tell us jokes, and one day they may even do a commencement address?

- Last, but not least . . . . Lewis Howard Latimer **added the carbon filament to Thomas Edison's lightbulb** (Edison originally used paper filaments that burned out quickly). The Latimer improvement gives us the bulbs we use to this day. Latimer also wrote the first book on incandescence AND went on to draft the patent drawings and notes for the telephone. He sold his works to a company that would become General Electric. Lewis Latimer also supervised the installation of public electric lights throughout New York, Philadelphia, Montreal and London. He was on the margins. His parents were former slaves in Virginia who escaped North in search of a better life.

Think about the likelihood of a person who was not even supposed to learn to read, inventing the filament for the lightbulb and drawing the patent filing for the telephone. Let that sink in. There are thousands of remarkable stories like this that have been kept from us. I pray that God forgives us for focusing more on lost causes than on finding needed cures. It's as if we are looking up for ideas and only choosing to see half the sky. The people on the margins should not be made invisible. What can we learn from these people who change the world for the better in spite of the obstacles? What their work tells me, is that the real genius in the world is in recognizing the genius in others. My hypothesis is that we all have the capacity to be great. God distributes talent generously throughout our species and all of us get to have the life we are willing to work for. It is in our naked self-interest to invest in everyone – every girl and every boy on the planet – because we have no idea where the cure for ALS is coming from. We have no idea where the cure for cancer is coming from. We have no idea where the cure for Alzheimer's is coming from. What we do know for sure is that the cures that will help your family and mine are randomly distributed somewhere out there in the world. What we do know for sure is that the person with the cure we need right now might just be listening to this message.

What we do know for sure is that the antidote for all that ails us is YOU. I challenge you to decide to be GREAT. Because if a person on the margins can achieve at the highest levels, what is our excuse for dabbling in mediocrity?

Before I invented anything; before writing my 8th book; before my AR firm won the top 7-figure prize for the 2020 global 5G challenge; before I ran a multi-billion dollar company for Verizon with over 40,000 employees; before I made my first movie with Lionsgate . . . I was a person on the margins. I almost flunked out of engineering school. It was reading about people like Mr. Latimer that changed my life. I realized that if he could change the world at the time he was alive with very few resources and limited support, I could change my trajectory if I applied myself. The stories of success and innovation helped me to stop seeing the world through a prism of sorrows. Instead, I learned to look at the world through the lens of achievement. This shift in my world view has made all the difference.

Life is a journey. When we learn better, we must do better. We do not get to choose where we start, but we do get to choose where we end up. I am thankful for all of those that sacrificed — every ethnicity and every gender — to show us what it means to be human and how the pursuit of excellence allows us to pay forward the gift of our very existence. Complaining about tough times, complaining about what we don't have, blaming everyone else for what we have failed to do as people is an inadequate contribution to the future of our success.

Yes, I chair 7 companies and I still read every day and at times work into the wee hours of the morning. When the curious ask why I work so much as a retired person and why I send e-mails at 3 and 4am . . . , I tell them that I work while they sleep, so I can live like they dream. Innovators are curious people. We seek understanding as we find our place in the world. I have learned to set aside excuses. I exist to find the opportunities in life that bring me joy. What I also have learned is that the world is full of opportunities and the best innovators know how to create opportunities as well. You are innovators. "Start where you are. Use what you have. Do what you can." Arthur Ashe said that. It's good advice.

Did you know that Steven Spielberg has dyslexia? So does Cher, Tim Tebow, Keira Knightley, Whoopie Goldberg, Adam Leipzig, Daniel Radcliffe and Anderson Cooper. Albert Einstein, JFK, George Washington and even Leonardo di Vinci also had dyslexia. Did you know Justin Timberlake has ADHD? So does Lisa Ling. What is my point? These ailments did not hold any of these talented human beings back from becoming the best version of themselves. In fact, one could argue that they learned to use their challenges to soar. Consider this . . . people who are dyslexic have an extraordinary ability to solve problems. In fact, according to Professor Julie Logan, professor of entrepreneurship at the Cass Business School in London, 35% of the entrepreneurs she surveyed across the United States identified themselves as dyslexic. Her study concluded that "dyslexics were more likely than nondyslexics to delegate authority, excel in oral communication and problem solving and were twice as likely to own two or more businesses." I think I am a little bit dyslexic and I'm OK with that. My Wife may say I am completely dyslexic and she's OK with that? Thank you honey.

I find it interesting that the people that give the most, are often the people that have the least.

I'm reminded of a picture of Albert Einstein that hangs in my office. It's an image of the great scientist giving a private lecture to a small class of African American men at Lincoln

University (an HBCU).   The esteemed scientist rarely gave guest lectures, so I was puzzled why he regularly agreed to give lectures to these young men on the margins. A few months ago, the President of Norfolk State University (where I serve on the Board of Trustees) shared a Washington Post article with me that made everything more clear. You see, during WWII, German Jews were having difficulty getting visas into the United States – there was a law called the "public charge" policy that required immigrants to prove they would not become a burden on the nation before they were allowed in. The prevailing US policy was an effective death sentence for many German Jews. It turns out that HBCUs (not the more prestigious Universities or the US Government) gave jobs to Jewish scholars to help them make their way to safety in the United States and away from the Holocaust. Einstein was a German Jew. He knew this history, and respected the sacrifice and courage of the HBCUs to help his people on the margins. Many lives were saved because of this courage. Einstein was simply paying the kindness forward. He did not forget those on the margins.

Let me close with Leonardo da Vinci. The man for whom your program is named was also a person on the margins. I already told you that he had dyslexia. Did you know that he was also born out of wedlock; that's right . . . illegitimate? Did you know that his orphaned mother was no more than 16 years old when she gave birth to him? He was the oldest of 12 siblings. Did you know that he was born impoverished and he had no formal education? He was also jailed briefly because some did not agree with his choice of life companions – yes, . . . he loved those on the margins? From these humble beginnings, da Vinci became a great painter and one of the world's great minds – considered a bonified polymath – or multi-talented genius and renaissance man. His "Mona Lisa" is the most recognized portrait in the world. The Last Supper is the most reproduced religious painting of all time. And his Salvator Mundi is the most expensive painting ever sold at public auction – it was purchased in 2017 for almost $500 million dollars! This year, for the first time, the Louvre in Paris opened 24/7 on weekends so more visitors could see the final days of the otherwise sold out da Vinci exhibit. The exhibit opened on Oct 24 to celebrate the 500th anniversary of da Vinci's death. The exhibit of drawings and paintings shattered the museum's attendance record with over one million visitors stopping by to see the collection of works by the great Renaissance man.

So what is the point of all of this meandering through history? Let me tell you. If you think lights are important; if you think fresh produce is important; if you think getting your mail or having GPS is important; if you think open heart surgery is important; if you think art is important; if you think your phone, rocket fuel, computers, and space flight are among the important contributions to the story of humanity; know that all of these things were created by people on the margins. Accordingly, I respectfully ask that when you leave this place today and for the rest of your lives, . . . pay the lessons you have learned here forward by choosing to be excellent and remembering those on the margins.

Congratulations – da Vinci class of 2020. You have earned this graduation and no one can take that away. Become the change you seek.

Thank you.

Note: This graduation address was initially prepared for delivery to 300 students at the VCU da Vinci Center graduation set for May 7, 2020. However, due to the Coronavirus Pandemic of 2020, the speech was reworked for video delivery to all the graduates, their families and the University Community. Special Thanks to Jackie Stone, Queon "Q" Martin, Sim Stevenson, Monty Ross, Nick Powell and Jordan Faett for their work to review the text, prepare the video presentation and develop the original music score in time for graduation.

THE DIVINE PUZZLE OF LIFE: AS SEEN BY A NATIVE SON OF VIRGINIA

Our Nation has not yet fully addressed its original sin . . . the savage institution of slavery. The residue of inequality still permeates our shores and infects the globe as a pandemic of the mind. Despite our scientific similarities (we are more alike than different), when it comes to power - both its use and restraint - in 2020 we still run into a refrain of white resistance and the oddity of white frailty. These two pillars of privilege shape a misinformed, yet powerful world view of the pecking order of humanity that we all experience in contemporary America and beyond.

Over the course of 50+ years of being American and Virginian, I have learned that we are all simply human beings sharing the same rock. I try to teach my children and friends who will listen that we are all cousins trying to find our way home. I also teach my sons that while they should enjoy the same rights and privileges as others, the reality is that the sickness created by a culture that would rather teach lies about Christopher Columbus than acknowledge truths about Lewis H. Latimer (the Virginian son of runaway slaves who invented the filament for the present day lightbulb), means they exist in a world that does not always protect the value of their humanity. A culture that overplays white contributions and underplays the contributions of people of color will underplay the importance of who they are as young black men. The educational and political systems of our Land, formal and informal, have too often perpetuated a Eurocentric indoctrination of humanity versus teaching critical thinking. It is up to civil society to close the gap between the two. This is where the "truth" lives . . . in the gap.

How I wish we could see ourselves as part of a *divine puzzle of life*. In this puzzle, we are all essential pieces. Our respective contributions are important and unique to the puzzle. We all add value. What is clear with this framing of life, is that a person has to know who he or she is so that they know where they fit in the puzzle. It is critically important to know your place in the world before you can determine what you must do in the world.

> You can't know your place unless you know who you are. In America, we pretend that African-American history started in Virginia in 1619. We tell every child in school this fiction.

We tell them how Christopher Columbus discovered America. He did not. We leave out of the American story almost every important contribution from non-whites and go further to erect monuments and give platitudes for characters in our history who in fact tried to tear up our more perfect union and subjugate black men and women to the horrors of chattel slavery. Our schools do not teach us that when black men and women played by the rules and built up banks, and schools, and self-sufficient communities like in Tulsa, Oklahoma, those cities were literally bombed and burned to the ground by angry whites, often for the trumped up charge of an offense against a white woman. If we only told the truth, we could mitigate these atrocities and tragic mishaps of humanity and press on to a world where each citizen (each piece in the divine puzzle) could develop without the pathology of indoctrination and contribute beyond the basic instinct to survive.

When we all come into the full knowledge of who we are, we will know where we fit in the divine puzzle of life.

Is it too early in 2020 to be honest in America? Is white frailty so entrenched in our white brothers and sisters minds that they can't handle the truth? I think not. The streets of America and other cities around the world are filled with protestors of all ethnicities precisely because we have all been lied to. The lynching of George Floyd and the murder of many other innocents have brought us to a tipping point. For the sake of our sons and daughters, I hope things will never be the same.

It's time for the truth America.

As we emerge from this global pandemic, may we also emerge from the systemic pandemics of hatred and fear fueled by the contagious pedagogy of white supremacy. It is time for real change.

The truth will set us free.

This article was first published in Beacon's Rebellion and in Maria Shriver's Sunday Paper.

BK FULTON, P.G.A - CHAIRMAN & CEO OF SOULIDIFLY PRODUCTIONS

BK is the chairman of 7 companies and an award-winning filmmaker and author. In 2017 BK founded Soulidifly Productions - a film, stage and TV investment company designed to promote a more inclusive narrative in media. The company has produced 15 feature films, 15 books and two #1 shows on Broadway since its inception, including the highest grossing August Wilson show and revival of all time. Soulidifly is the creator of the *Blueprint Script & Media Prize* and owns SoulVision Magazine, SoulVision.TV and Body Snatchers Productions. The company retains ownership interests in MoviePass 2.0 (films, gaming, and B2B), *Iconic Events Releasing* (over 8,000 screens), and MediaU.com (the first online film school with university transcripts) among other ventures. BK is also a principal with Ralph Sampson and Jim Franklin in *Winner's Circle Ventures* – a $100 million dollar strategic investment company targeting all entrepreneurs, especially women and minorities.

Prior to becoming a full-time author and entrepreneur, BK was Vice President of the Mid-Atlantic Region for Verizon Communications, Inc. and President of Verizon Virginia and West Virginia. He has held senior leadership, media, technology, and policy development posts with the U.S. Department of Commerce, AOL, Time Warner, Verizon, and the National Urban League. BK is considered one of the most influential African Americans in technology. He is a Computerworld-Smithsonian Laureate (2000) and his influential writings on technology and the underserved are permanently archived at the Smithsonian Institution. His board service includes Norfolk State University, TowneBank, the Library of Virginia Foundation, Media Mentors, The Jamestown-Yorktown Foundation and MediaU.com. He was most recently inducted into the JA Business Hall of Fame (2022).

BK holds a Bachelor's degree from Virginia Tech, a Master of Science degree and Sloan Fellowship from Harvard and the New School, and a Juris Doctorate from New York Law School. He is married to Mrs. Jacquleyn E. Stone, a Harvard Law graduate and prominent Richmond attorney at the McGuireWoods law firm. Jackie and BK are co-parents to three young men – Joshua, Terrell, and Sam.

CPSIA information can be obtained
at www.ICGtesting.com
Printed in the USA
LVHW071043240723
753168LV00096B/171/J